RACING CHAMPION

RACING CHAMPION

DESERT ORCHID

John Dorman

INTRODUCTION
BY SIMON SHERWOOD

THE CROWOOD PRESS

Printed and bound in Great Britain
by The Bath Press

Typeset by Macdonald Lindsay Pindar plc, Edinburgh

British Library Cataloguing in Publication Data
Dorman, John
  Racing champion—Desert Orchid.
  1. Steeplechasing horses. Desert Orchid
  I. Title
  798.4'5

  ISBN 1—85223—381—8

ACKNOWLEDGEMENTS

I would like to thank Colin Brown, David Elsworth and Simon Sherwood for all the help they have given me while researching and writing this book. My thanks are also due to Christopher Forster for his constant encouragement and support.

PHOTO ACKNOWLEDGEMENTS

The author and publisher would like to thank the following sources for use of their photographs:

Trevor Jones, pages 9, 33, 40/41, 44/45, 48, 102/103, 104/105, 106/107, 123; George Selwyn, pages 10 (top), 12, 13, 15, 17, 18, 24, 25, 29, 33, 39, 57, 59, 66, 71, 77, 89, 126/127; Gerry and Mark Cranham, pages 10 (bottom), 36/37, 50/51, 65, 87, 112; Alan Johnson, pages 23, 42/43, 53, 55, 72, 73, 134/135; Bernard Parkin, pages 34, 35, 97, 98, 99, 108/109; John Rogers/Katz Eyes, pages 38, 100, 101; Kenneth Bright, pages 46/47; Roger Linge, page 79; Sporting Pictures (UK), pages 83, 110/111; Michael Steele/*The Independent*, pages 94/95; Chris Smith/*The Sunday Times*, pages 114/115, 118/119.

CONTENTS

To Irene, with love

Preface

It was, to say the least, an incongruous scenario. Gathered in the hotel car park, in warm spring sunshine, a small group of people appeared in various stages of disarray. Jimmy Burridge, Desert Orchid's breeder, and his wife Midge, Hugh and Suzanne Roberts, the hotel's proprietors, half a dozen guests.

Hugh Roberts poured champagne into the small gold trophy. It was passed silently around, with the reverence of a communion chalice. One by one, each person drank from it, then held it up, glowing in the sunlight, to read the inscription: The Tote Cheltenham Gold Cup 1989. Passengers in passing cars peered curiously. If they had known what was going on, there would have been a traffic jam on the Fosseway.

Twenty-four hours earlier it had been snowing. Twenty-four hours earlier the Burridges had been agonising over whether or not to run the horse. It was David Elsworth, convinced that Desert Orchid was the best in the race, who finally tipped the balance. Some four hours later, as the grey fought his way home, Cheltenham had resounded to a roar never likely to be repeated. The old saying: 'You've got to be in it to win it', had never been more memorably vindicated.

Slowly, reluctantly, the group began to disperse. The Gold Cup was packed into its special case and put in the boot of the car, to be driven home to Leicestershire. It was time to get back to reality, after twenty-four hours of living a dream. No-one there, that day, would ever forget the dream, but Suzanne Roberts took photographs anyway, just to make sure. . . .

Introduction

by Simon Sherwood

WHEN DAVID ELSWORTH offered me the ride on either Combs Ditch or Desert Orchid—whichever one Colin Brown rejected—in the 1986 King George VI Chase, I wasn't really bothered which horse I rode. Although beaten only a neck by Wayward Lad in the previous year's race, Combs Ditch had not run since, and Desert Orchid had never before tackled the three mile trip. To be honest, I had been hoping to get the ride on Bolands Cross, but when his trainer Nick Gaselee availed himself of the services of the champion jockey Peter Scudamore, and Colin chose Combs Ditch on the morning of the race, I set about acquainting myself with the grey horse.

In fact, David Elsworth told me before the race that he thought Colin had picked the wrong horse. He was convinced that Desert Orchid would win if he got the trip, and he was also convinced that he would get the trip. He was right, of course, and the race itself has passed into jumping folklore. It was the most wonderful spare ride that any jockey could hope for, bowling along in front, the horse jumping perfectly, and coming home 20 lengths clear, knowing that there was still something left in the tank. Desert Orchid already had quite a following, but I think it was that race that really established him as the people's favourite.

Although I no longer ride him, people still ask me what it is that makes him so popular, and I find it hard to define. He is a grey, of course, but there is also just something about that horse that makes him a little bit different. He has charisma; the public flock to see because of it, and when you walk into the paddock to ride him he has that aura around him. He has a wonderful outlook, dark eyes, big ears, and a very arrogant, almost athletic walk. You know that from a jockey's view as soon as you get on him you're going to

Simon Sherwood. Twice Champion Amateur Jockey, runner-up to Peter Scudamore in his first season as a professional, considered by many to be the best of his time. He has always been at pains to point out that Colin Brown was responsible for the initial development of Desert Orchid. 'I got on him at the time when all his kinks had been ironed out by Colin.'

9

THE 1986
KING GEORGE—
Simon Sherwood
Desert Orchid jumps
the last.
'I remember going to
the last thinking
"right, we've got
this race sewn up:
he only has to jump
it." He met it a little
short and just
popped into it, and
when he landed he
was a little slow
getting away from
it. In that situation
you think "My God,
someone might be
coming with a
rattle," but there
was no danger.
There won't be
many easier
victories of a race of
that calibre.'

have a lovely ride. He's going to look after you and he's going to try his hardest, so you have tremendous respect for him. Even watching a piece of film about him on television at home cuts right through me—there is something just a little bit extraordinary about him.

Colin Brown did all the major preparation work on Desert Orchid, first schooling him over hurdles when he was a three-year-old. When I took over on him the horse was very much more the finished article. Before I ever sat on him I prejudged him a bit on what I had seen, and I had the feeling he was a pretty hairy, headstrong, brave horse who jumped flat out, and the jockey just acted as a passenger and with a bit of luck you jumped the fences. But I soon learned that there was more to him than that. He was quick, he was accurate, and he responded to sympathetic riding.

I also believe that he is an extremely intelligent animal. When we were involved in that desperately close finish with Panto Prince in the Victor Chandler Chase at Ascot in 1988, Desert Orchid moved across and almost ran into Panto Prince, and I had to correct him. Then, he leaned right. At Cheltenham, in the Gold Cup, I had my stick in my right hand prepared for this, but he went left towards Yahoo and I had to correct him. I genuinely believe that on both occasions he went for the other horse, as if to say, 'You're beating me—get out of the way!' To me, that shows the intelligence of the horse.

My brother Oliver also believes that Desert Orchid was responsible for destroying the confidence of another horse to such an extent that it never again fulfilled its true potential. Oliver was assistant trainer to Fred Winter at the time, and they had a top class horse in the yard called I Haventalight. The two horses met in the Foodbrokers Armour Novice Hurdle at Kempton on Boxing Day 1983, the only time Richard Linley rode

Richard Linley's record on Desert Orchid was one ride, one win, when he deputised for Colin Brown in the Foodbroker Armour Novice Hurdle at Kempton on Boxing Day 1983. The pair are pictured jumping the last flight.

Desert Orchid. John Francome was on I Haventalight, but Desert Orchid jumped off and made all, skating up by 15 lengths, and Fred was annoyed because he felt his was the better horse, and that John had not given it a very good ride.

A fortnight later the two met in the Tolworth Hurdle at Sandown, and Fred gave John instructions to sit on Desert Orchid's heels all the way and pounce on him at the last. But Desert Orchid, with Colin back on board, won by eight lengths, and Oliver maintains that I Haventalight was never the same horse again.

There is a story, which I believe is true, that after that race David Elsworth was standing in the gents toilet minding his own business when he felt a piercing gaze on him. He turned round and there was Fred Winter looking at him steely-eyed, and before David could say anything, Fred said: 'That *is* a bloody good horse, isn't it?'

After the 1986 King George, Richard Burridge, that

most loyal of owners and a man whose primary concern for Desert Orchid is the horse's welfare, ensured that Colin Brown resumed riding the horse regularly, which was quite right and proper. However, when Colin retired at the end of the 1988 Cheltenham Festival meeting, I was asked to take over the ride, and of course I did not hesitate. Desert Orchid and I had the most wonderful partnership—nine wins from ten races, including two King Georges, the Whitbread Gold Cup and the Cheltenham Gold Cup. What more could a jockey ask for? I am also satisfied, in my own heart of hearts, that although we fell at Liverpool our unbeaten partnership has been retained. If Desert Orchid had finished that day he would have finished a tired fourth or fifth, which would not have been a genuine result, and I am glad that instead he had the fall and got away with it. Two days later I rode The Thinker in the Grand National and we finished third, but with all due respect to The Thinker's connections, even if we had won that

Desert Orchid and Panto Prince (Brendan Powell), jump the last in the Victor Chandler in tandem.

Simon Sherwood: 'That was the least enjoyable ride I had on Desert Orchid, because Brendan took us on from the first. Nothing was very fluent about the race. We gave Panto Prince a stone and a half, and it was a real fight from the second last.'

day it would not have matched the thrill of winning the Gold Cup on Desert Orchid.

Talking about horses like The Thinker, another previous Gold Cup winner, I have occasionally tried to compare Desert Orchid with some of the other very good horses I was lucky enough to ride. It's not easy. Barnbrook Again, I have always thought, was potentially a better horse than Desert Orchid, but that potential has not yet been fulfilled. Even so, Desert Orchid makes up for that by having greater guts, and his heart is in a better place.

Brown Chamberlain was a lovely horse, but unfortunately I never rode him at the height of his talent.

But I have never sat on anything that could compare with Desert Orchid at all. He is an all-round jockey's dream. He jumps well, he's honest, he tries his hardest and he is a very easy horse to ride between the fences.

Increasingly throughout his career, and especially during last season, Desert Orchid has done a tremendous amount of good for the public image of jump racing. He deserves to go on jumping fences for as long as he enjoys it—and enjoy it he certainly does—and the public deserves to watch him at it. I have been lucky enough to ride some very good horses in my time, but I can genuinely say that Desert Orchid is one of the few horses who can get under your skin a bit. He means more to you than just a mere racehorse.

Richard Dunwoody is in for an experience he will never forget, and I wish him all the best.

Desert Orchid at his imperious best in the Racecall Gainsborough Chase at Sandown on 4 February, when he had to concede over a stone to the Mackeson-winner, Pegwell Bay.
Simon Sherwood: 'From a riding point of view this was one of his most impressive performances. He gave Pegwell Bay a fair bit of weight. Desert Orchid led on the first circuit, and Pegwell Bay went ahead on the railway fences second time round. Then we came on terms with him again.'

In the beginning

***

FOR A HORSE who was to go on to lift nearly every major prize in steeplechasing, to become the leading money winner in the sport's history, and to become the nation's favourite racehorse, Desert Orchid's family background was, in terms of results, undistinguished, although the free-running spirit was already evident.

James Burridge found Desert Orchid's granddam, Grey Orchid, in a field near Newark when the horse was a five-year-old. He decided she would make a suitable hunter and paid £175 for her, but when he took her home she proved to be almost impossibly headstrong. The first time Burridge mounted her she immediately threw him off, and he was saved from serious injury only by a heap of manure. On the second occasion she galloped explosively round a field, throwing her head back into the rider's face. It was not an auspicious start.

But Burridge persisted, and eventually won a point-to-point on her, before deciding to breed from the mare. After one unsuccessful mating she was paired with a stallion named Brother, from the Hunters' Improvement Society, and the result was Flower Child, Desert Orchid's mother.

In the hunting field, Flower Child demonstrated the same headstrong, free-running character as her mother, outpacing and outjumping some of the best hunters in the county. Like Desert Orchid in later years, she simply loved running. Eventually James Burridge, now retired, found her too much of a handful, and she was sent point-to-pointing at the comparatively late age of eight.

Again, Flower Child displayed all the characteristics that would later be associated with her son. She always wanted to make the running, she jumped her fences with a bravado bordering on foolishness, and she often tired

David Elsworth. A forthright man and a brilliant trainer. As well as being responsible for Desert Orchid he also trained Rhyme 'N' Reason to win the 1988 Grand National. Champion trainer 1987/88 season.

well before the end of her races. But James Burridge was sufficiently impressed to send her into training, at an age when most mares would have already had foals at stud.

Flower Child was sent to Charlie James's yard near Lambourn. When she was schooled over fences she appeared to be more interested in jumping the post and rails surrounding the schooling field. James was not over-impressed with her all-round ability, but he had to admit that she was a great trier. In three seasons she won two minor chases, and fell only once, at the Chair fence at Aintree in what was then the Topham Trophy.

At the very late age of eleven, in 1978, Flower Child was retired by James Burridge to the paddocks. She had all the right ingredients for a broodmare: she was consistent and competitive, and she loved jumping. Burridge paid £350 for her first covering, by Grey Mirage, who as a three-year-old on the flat had started third favourite in the 1972 2000 Guineas, but finished unplaced, ridden by Lester Piggott. By coincidence,

Grey Mirage was trained at Whitsbury by Colin Brown's brother-in-law, Tom Marshall. He never won over distances of more than 7 furlongs. Speed was his finest attribute.

The result of this pairing was Desert Orchid, born in 1979. He was taken to the Burridge estate near Melton Mowbray, where he soon turned out to be even bigger and stronger, and at least as lively as his mother. He once escaped from his paddock and galloped loose on a busy main road for twenty-five minutes, miraculously without coming to any harm. When he was broken in as a three-year-old he displayed all the strong-willed, high-spirited characteristics shown by his mother and grandmother in earlier years. But it was a visit to James Burridge by his son, Richard, which sparked off the start of Desert Orchid's remarkable climb to the top of the steeplechasing tree.

Father and son were inspecting the young grey in a field, and Richard was not very impressed. The horse was, he thought, scraggy and uncoordinated. Suddenly, however, perhaps stung by a bee, Desert Orchid took off across the field at full gallop. The younger Burridge realised immediately what a wonderful mover he was, what immense potential he had. Virtually on the spot he negotiated a 50% controlling interest in the horse, with his father retaining 25% and Simon Bullimore, a family friend, the other 25%. It was probably one of the most momentous decisions of Richard Burridge's life.

In 1982 it was decided to put Desert Orchid in training. The question was where, and with whom. Richard Burridge, who lives a solitary existence high on the Yorkshire Moors, wanted Desert Orchid trained in equal isolation, rather than at one of the busy centres like Lambourn, where numerous trainers' strings are queuing up behind one another to get on the gallops. He chose David Elsworth.

Elsworth, then in his early forties, has turned out to be one of the most successful trainers of the 1980s, being champion trainer of the 1987/88 jumping season, the year he won the Grand National with Rhyme 'N' Reason. As a professional National Hunt jockey between 1957 and 1972 he was perfectly capable but not very successful. After riding for a variety of trainers he became assistant to Lt-Col. Ricky Vallance, and he soon began to display his prodigious talents for preparing horses for the big occasion. It was Elsworth who orchestrated Red Candle's victory in the Mackeson Gold Cup, and later in the Hennessy Gold Cup, when the horse beat Red Rum.

However, when Vallance lost his licence, Elsworth was out of a job, with a young wife and family to support. For a time he worked as a stall-holder at the West Country markets, but, like most people in racing, the bug never left him. In 1977 he started a livery yard in the village of Figheldean on the edge of Salisbury Plain, and applied for his own licence the following year.

It did not take long for the talented trainer to taste success, and he moved to larger stables at Lucknam Park near Chippenham. Soon, however, with an expanding string on both the flat and over the jumps, even bigger premises were required, and Elsworth moved again to where he trains today: Whitsbury, near Fordingbridge in Hampshire.

Sir Gordon Richards once trained at the Whitsbury Estate. It is a huge, superbly equipped yard, and the gallops, with their magnificent views over the Hampshire Downs, would be difficult to better anywhere in the country. And in racing terms it is isolated: Elsworth's nearest fellow-trainer is Toby

Balding at Weyhill, some ten miles away. Richard Burridge made an inspired choice.

Desert Orchid arrived at Whitsbury in the autumn of 1982. He immediately showed his character by refusing to come out of his horsebox, and Elsworth only finally succeeded by leading him backwards down the ramp. He then refused to enter his stable, and again Elsworth had to coax him through the door in reverse. In those days he was almost iron-grey in colour, and apart from his initial eccentricities he made no deeper impression on Elsworth than any other horse arriving at the yard.

'When he first came he wasn't anything exceptional. He was a well-made little horse but ideally I'd have liked him to be a little bit bigger. He was a grey and I like greys, but that fact wouldn't have made any difference looking at it objectively.'

Another arrival at Whitsbury at around the same time as Desert Orchid was Rodney Boult, who joined David Elsworth as head lad. Hugely experienced, sympathetic and skilful, Boult came from John Dunlop's Arundel yard, where he regularly rode the 1978 Derby winner Shirley Heights at work. The lad assigned to look after Desert Orchid on a day-to-day basis was Gary Morgan, a young, 7-stone apprentice.

The team was coming together. It was now time for Desert Orchid to be introduced to his jockey.　□

The first hurdles

COLIN BROWN is a cheerful, likeable energetic man with a word—usually a good word—for everyone and every occasion. Now a successful publican near Hungerford he was in the early 1980s a busy freelance jockey who rode most of David Elsworth's jumpers. Shortly after Desert Orchid's arrival at Whitsbury, Elsworth rang Brown to tell him about the newcomer to the yard.

'I remember David laughing and saying, "You should see this thing the Burridges have sent us. About 15 hands, a fat, round, roly-poly grey thing!"' In later years a remark like that would have been treated as heresy.

When Brown sat on the grey for the first time he immediately had reason for a little guarded optimism. The horse showed signs of going very well, the sort of signs that indicate to both jockey and trainer that they might have a bit of a machine on their hands, but maybe one which, like Desert Orchid's father, will only last six or seven furlongs. Then Brown popped him over a few hurdles.

'He was so quick and accurate. A natural. He went over four hurdles just like he'd been doing it all his life. We never schooled him over hurdles again. He was so good.'

David Elsworth has always maintained a reputation for running his horses in decent races at Group 1 tracks, and Desert Orchid was no exception. He first appeared in public on 21 January 1983 in the Walton Novices Hurdle at Kempton Park. In a field containing several experienced handicappers from the flat, the unknown grey drifted to 50-1 in the betting. As Colin Brown recalls, it was not an auspicious debut.

'As I went down to the start on him he was very strong. I thought: "Crikey, this is going to be a bit hairy! I know he jumps well but I'm not sure that I'm going

Desert Orchid and Rodney Boult on the Whitsbury gallops, followed by Ross Arnott and Barnbrook Again. Simon Sherwood has always maintained that Barnbrook Again is the only horse he has ever sat on who was potentially as good as Desert Orchid.

to be able to hold him!''

'We went a very fast gallop but he was still pulling double. At the fourth hurdle Robert Stronge had a fall and Desert Orchid picked up outside the wing and landed on his head, and all I could think about for the next two flights was that I must have killed Robert!'

Stronge, in fact, survived with a severe headache, saved by his helmet. Brown, meanwhile, still had his hands full:

'Three out and I was still pulling double. We moved through the field to about fourth position and then he got very tired. We went to the last—and he's such a brave horse—but he couldn't come up when he wanted to and he put down and just fell through the hurdle.'

For the next twenty minutes most people on the racecourse, including James Burridge and Gary Morgan, thought they had seen the first and last of Desert Orchid in action. He lay prostrate on the ground, and Brown took his tack off him. Contrary to popular myth, the dreaded green screens that signify the presence of the vet's bullet were never erected, though the vet did warn Burridge that he might have to do just that. Eventually, the badly winded horse got up, and Brown, who had always believed that this was the only problem, summed up the occasion very succinctly:

'He was knackered.'

The Kempton experience seemed to unnerve his connections more than it did the horse. Desert Orchid went home, ate his supper, and was his usual ebullient self the next morning. Later, in conversation with James Burridge, David Elsworth summed up the character of the horse by explaining that while it is often difficult to extract 95% effort from some horses, it is equally difficult to prevent Desert Orchid from giving 105%.

Desert Orchid ran again a month later, in the Mere

Maiden Hurdle at Wincanton. Although unplaced, he settled a lot better and jumped well, before tiring towards the end of the race. After a break of only a fortnight, Elsworth sent him to Sandown to contest the Lilac Novice Hurdle. It was his first visit to the course that many people still associate primarily with the great horse. He took on older horses for the first time and was backed down to 7-1; Brown remembers that it was an encouraging run:

'After his first couple of races we thought we'd let him run from the front, and at Sandown he made all the running. Three out he looked cooked, but he kept on running up the hill, and we were beaten only by a neck by Steve Smith Eccles on Diamond Hunter. I didn't hit him, and I didn't give him a hard race.'

Desert Orchid's final run of that first campaign was on 25 March at Newbury, his first experience of a left-hand track which, in years to come, was to provoke great debate about just how well the horse could handle them. Even at that stage of his career, Colin Brown had fairly firm feelings on the subject:

'I remember that going down the back straight he was jumping a bit right and hanging a bit right, and I said to David and the owners after the race that he really wants to go right-handed. We were unplaced, and that was it for the season.'

Nevertheless, after the heart-stopping fall at Kempton, it had been a fairly encouraging first season, and Brown already knew that the potential was there:

'I thought he was going to be quite good because he was just so accurate at everything he did. He jumped beautifully at home and although he was a bit tearaway I could see he was going to be quite exciting. Providing everything went well I though he had a bit of potential—which he obviously did turn out to have!' □

Winning ways

BY THE AUTUMN of 1983 Gary Morgan had left Whitsbury in search of better opportunities for rides, and Desert Orchid had a new groom in the shape of Jackie Parrish. The rest of the team remained unchanged, and Desert Orchid was sent out for his first race of the season on firm ground at Ascot on 29 October, in the Haig Whisky Novice Hurdle. David Elsworth, impressed by the way the horse had been working at home, was confident he would have the measure of the rest of the field, which included Lucky Rascal, trained by Josh Gifford and owned by the sporting Peter Hopkins.

'The second season I had Desert Orchid I realised he might be something special. Before he went to Ascot he was giving us some very strong signals. Peter Hopkins asked me how I thought we'd run, and I told him we'd win, and Peter said, "Well, yours will have to be a bit useful, because Josh is very sweet on ours."'

Desert Orchid was 'a bit useful' that day. He tackled the first two flights of hurdles as though he was running in a 5-furlong sprint, and although he tied up a bit on the final bend, he trounced Lucky Rascal by 20 lengths. Elsworth was impressed: 'It was then that I began to realise that he was probably very good indeed.'

Three weeks later Desert Orchid returned to Ascot to contest the Bingley Novices Hurdle, again on firm ground. He started favourite at 2-1 on, and the only threat from the three-horse field was likely to come from Don Giovanni, ridden by John Francome. But Colin Brown was unconcerned:

'Franc lined up beside me. He wasn't going to let me go. But by the time we reached the first we were away. He jumped very accurately, and he skated up by fifteen lengths.'

By now, Desert Orchid had begun to settle down

Jackie Parrish

better in his races, and Brown found him a much easier ride when he let him bowl along in front, something the horse obviously loved doing. Those first two races had been over 2 miles, but Elsworth felt he was now ready for longer distances. He sent him to Sandown on 2 December for the December Novices Hurdle, over 2 miles 5 furlongs. Desert Orchid started 6-5 on favourite, but the final few yards over the extra distance caught him out. He was collared, close to home, by Richard Rowe on Catchphrase, but Brown was nevertheless pleased with the effort:

'We made all the running and I tried to conserve his

energy, and he relaxed a lot better. Going to the last down the back I wasn't sure how he was going to finish up the hill, but he stayed on very well. We were only beaten in the final 100 yards or so, which was a very good run over two miles five for the first time.'

It was indeed. Desert Orchid sometimes seemed to gain lengths over his pursuers in the air, and there was no question about the stamina of Catchphrase. The Josh Gifford-trained horse had already won over 3 miles, and was also a year older than Desert Orchid.

In the Foodbrokers' Armour Novices Hurdle on 26 December, Desert Orchid reverted to 2 miles, and for the first time was not ridden by Colin Brown. Boxing Day, like Easter Monday and bank holidays, sees a plethora of jump meetings up and down the country, and any jockey in demand has a difficult decision to make. David Elsworth's useful handicapper Buckbe was running at Wincanton the same day, and Brown was under a certain amount of pressure to ride the mare from her owners, the Torys. He had also been offered the ride on King's Bishop by Les Kennard. Jockeys are primarily concerned about winners, no matter who they are or where they are. Brown, assured by Richard Burridge that he would ride Desert Orchid again next time out, went to Wincanton. Richard Linley substituted.

Desert Orchid, as usual, made all. Unconcerned about the change of jockey, he won by 15 lengths, having gone off as the 7-4 favourite. Meanwhile, Brown's decision to go to Wincanton was vindicated, as he won on both Buckbe and King's Bishop.

It was at that Kempton meeting on Boxing Day that an interesting piece of racing folklore began, when Oliver Sherwood, then assistant trainer to Fred Winter, swore that Desert Orchid was responsible for totally demoralising another horse.

The 5-2 second favourite that day was Fred Winter's I Haventalight, an ex-Irish gelding reckoned to be the most promising horse in the yard. Winter was annoyed that John Francome had let Desert Orchid get so far in front, and when the pair next met, in the Tolworth Hurdle at Sandown on 7 January, Winter gave Francome strict instructions to sit on Desert Orchid's tail all the way and produce I Haventalight at the last. Elsworth has happy memories of the occasion:

'I Haventalight was probably Fred's best young horse at the time, and he certainly thought it was better than Desert Orchid. He said to John: "Don't you let him get away this time," but we thrashed him again.

'Afterwards I was standing in the gents, and I felt this piercing gaze on me. I turned round, and there was Fred glaring at me, and he said "That *is* a bloody good horse of yours isn't it?"'

At Ascot, on 8 February 1984, Desert Orchid gained an 8-length but somewhat facile win over Hill's Pageant, after which it was decided to enter him for the Kingwell Pattern Hurdle at Wincanton on 23 February. This race has long been considered as a trial for the Champion Hurdle at Cheltenham, and the field that day included smart hurdlers of the likes of Stans Pride, Prideaux Boy and Very Promising. Desert Orchid took them all on, shook off the challenge of Stans Pride on the downhill run to the final flight, and won by 4 lengths. It was a brilliant display of jumping against some high-class opponents, and the bookmakers began to take notice. Before that Wincanton race, David Elsworth had backed Desert Orchid each way at 66-1 for the Champion Hurdle. Afterwards his odds tumbled to 14-1. On the day of the race itself they were down to 7-1.

Dawn Run took on Desert Orchid in the 1984

Champion Hurdle and thrashed him. In terms of pure results on the day, it was probably the most comprehensive beating the grey is ever likely to experience. Despite leading briefly just before halfway, Desert Orchid was annihilated by the big, aggressive mare, ridden by the great Jonjo O'Neill. He eventually finished seventh, and Brown was at a loss to explain the defeat:

'We planned to jump off towards the outside because we knew he preferred to go right-handed. I knew Desert Orchid was fast but I've never been so fast in my life. Dawn Run just took us on, and by the time I jumped the second hurdle I knew we were beaten. She was cruising, and we were already struggling.'

Very Promising also finished in front of Desert Orchid that day, a reverse of the Wincanton form, and all in all it was a disappointing end to what had been a superbly promising season—eight races, six wins, one second, but unplaced in the Champion Hurdle. Many trainers would have been tempted to go over fences the following season, but David Elsworth is a patient man. Desert Orchid would have one more season over hurdles. Apart from Cheltenham, he had swept the board. His improvement had been remarkable. The following season was to prove a great deal tougher. □

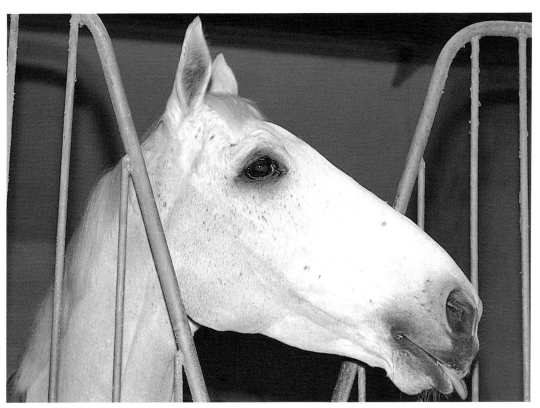

Desert Orchid at home in his box at Whitsbury—always an
interested observer in everything going on around him.

1984 CHAMPION HURDLE
Colin Brown: 'Jumping the second fence just behind Jonjo on Dawn Run.
David Elsworth said "make sure you pop him out of the gate pretty quick", and I
had him lined up. He always dwells a bit at the gate, but I had him walking
forward, had a good start, and I've never been so fast in my life!
'I remember jumping the first thinking, "well, everybody will take a pull in a
minute, because already I was off the bridle, and I couldn't believe how fast Dawn
Run was going—and so easily! By the time we jumped this fence I was already beaten!'

'A few fences later he'd made a couple of mistakes, and I wasn't going well, and I couldn't believe the way he was running. We put it down to going left-handed, but in hindsight I think Dawn Run was an exceptional horse, and Desert Orchid was not, at that stage, the horse he is now.'

Desert Orchid is clear of the field on the second circuit of the 1988 Whitbread Gold Cup. He went on to win by 2½ lengths.

Summer or winter, the work goes on.
Desert Orchid on the gallops at Whitsbury.

The 1988 Whitbread Gold Cup. Desert Orchid clears the Pond fence ahead of Kildimo and Strands of Gold.

LIVERPOOL, 6 APRIL 1989

Simon Sherwood

'The horse never felt happy in the race. He was jumping mostly to the right the whole way round and I was having quite a lot of trouble keeping him on the rails.

'We jumped the water for the last time and set off on the final circuit, and I wanted to quicken the pace because I could sense that there were a lot of horses coming right up behind me.

'As we went into the twelfth fence I thought "we're a little bit wrong, but nothing terrible", and I asked him to shorten a little bit. I didn't think we hit it very hard—I just felt he'd left his hind leg in it a bit—and then he went down.

'You would normally think "that's all right (pic. 3), but he just couldn't get himself right and suddenly crumbled. It was the fall of a tired horse.

'I stayed on board as long as I could, and he rolled right over me, but being a gentleman his back went over the top of me so no weight came on me at all. The expression on my face (pic. 8) is one of sheer disbelief that it had happened!'

46

Being led in after the Cheltenham Gold Cup, 1989. 'Janice came running along in floods of tears. I couldn't hear properly what Richard Burridge was saying at this point because there was such a noise from the people on the rails, but knowing him it was probably some philosophical comment!'

Chasing

IN THE LATE SPRING of 1985 Colin Brown schooled Desert Orchid over fences for the first time.

'He was brilliant. He simply flew over them. I think I only schooled him over fences once more after that.'

In October 1985 Desert Orchid was declared for both the Steel Plate & Sections Novice Chase and the Captain Quist Hurdle at Kempton. On the day, he ran in what was to be his last ever hurdle race, starting at 9-4 on. And fell, much to Brown's annoyance.

'We were 30 lengths clear turning into the straight, but once again he'd been blasé and careless about his hurdles. He just held off the second last, stood on it, and fell.'

The race was won by Wing and a Prayer, ridden by Simon Sherwood.

By now there was no further purchase in going hurdling, and David Elsworth set about turning Desert Orchid into a chaser. He was entered in the Woolea Lambskin Products Novice Chase at Devon and Exeter on 1 November, a race which Elsworth had won in the past with both Combs Ditch and Buckbe. He started 5-4 on favourite, but there was also strong support for Richard Linley's mount, Charcoal Wally, who had opened his chasing career with a win at the Kempton meeting a fortnight previously. This was another horse that liked to make the running, but the two jockeys were too experienced to try to take each other on.

'Richard and I are good pals, and we weren't going to cut each other's throats. Desert Orchid popped out the gate, flew the ditch, and after that he never made a mistake and won 20 lengths.'

It had been a stunning debut over fences, unexpectedly brilliant even by Desert Orchid's high standards, and several people predicted, after that one run, that here was a top-class chaser in the making.

Desert Orchid led from the start of the Trillium Handicap Hurdle at Ascot on 13 April, only to be undone by a careless mistake at the final flight. *Colin Brown:* 'He had 12 stone that day, and it was a good competitive hurdle race. Jonjo was riding Comedy Fair. He'd gone past me at the second last but at the last we were getting back and we'd just hit the front. Desert Orchid came up a fair way out and just clipped the top of the hurdle. Although he tried and tried he never really got his landing gear out, and over he went. 'We would have won that day. He jumped superbly and I thought "great, he's back to form". Then that happened.'

Encouraged by that spectacular first outing, David Elsworth ran the grey again in, in quick succession, the Hurst Park Novices Chase at Ascot, the Henry VIII Novices Chase at Sandown, and the Killiney Novices Chase, again at Ascot. Desert Orchid won them all with ease, by 12 lengths, 7 lengths and 20 lengths, displaying all the confident, front-running characteristics that had so endeared him to the racing public.

He and Colin Brown, now in their fourth season together, had developed into an excellent partnership. Brown was a tough, no-nonsense jump jockey who was prepared to take risks, especially going novice chasing on such a bold jumper as Desert Orchid. But he was also a sympathetic jockey, never hitting his horses unless he had to, and riding Desert Orchid over fences in that first season was not as difficult as it might have looked.

'I always found over the years, after his first few runs, that he was an easy ride. People said he must be a difficult ride, he pulls a lot and he jumps his fences so quickly, but I found him easy. He knew exactly what he was doing. He was the boss: you just had to steer him round.

'You had to judge the pace, which isn't always easy, but I was quite lucky on front runners. I seemed to ride them well, and I only got beaten on them a few times when I tried to press the button too early.'

Desert Orchid returned to Ascot on 10 January 1986 for the Thunder and Lightning Novices Chase. The only other two runners were John Edwards' smart young chaser Pearlyman, ridden by Paul Barton, and Charcoal Wally, this time with Graham McCourt up. Desert Orchid was the hot favourite at 11-4 on, although Pearlyman might not have been all that easy to beat on the day. In the event though, Brown ended up with the initials 'u.r.' (unseated rider) by his name. The blame, he

felt, lay with a television camera, which sounds most unlikely, although on this occasion he was quite justified.

After the horses turn out of the finishing straight at Ascot their progress on television is covered by a camera mounted on a car just inside the running rail, and this camera follows them all the way along the approach to Swinley Bottom. Brown recalls that going to the ditch Desert Orchid turned his head to look at the camera, and that he had to give him a slap to make him concentrate.

'He definitely spooked at the camera going down to Swinley Bottom, and he stood so far off the ditch that he landed on it. He started to scramble off, but then Charcoal Wally hit us up the backside and unseated me. Apart from when he fell at Liverpool that's the only time he's done so over fences.'

Both horse and jockey were unharmed, and they were back in action at Sandown on 1 February for the Scilly Isles Novice Chase. In yielding ground Desert Orchid was never able to establish supremacy over the mud-loving Berlin, trained by Nick Gaselee and ridden by Dermot Browne. The pair jumped the short-spaced railway fences side by side, but as they came up the final hill Berlin drew ahead by half a length, and Desert Orchid was unable to peg him back. It had, nevertheless, been an impressive performance in ground that the horse did not particularly like, although Colin Brown was not satisfied:

'We shouldn't have been beaten that day. He got a bit too close to the Pond fence, but I still feel we should have won.'

Desert Orchid's next target was Cheltenham, in the Arkle Challenge Trophy on the first day of the Festival meeting. He set a fast pace until three out, but again he

Desert Orchid leads over the first fence of the Henry VIII Novice Chase at Sandown on 30 November. On the far side is Ray Goldstein on Evening Song. 'Desert Orchid had his own way that day. He jumped well all the way and won easily.'

showed his comparative dislike for left-handed tracks by drifting and jumping right, thus giving away ground. Coming up the hill he was caught by both Oregon Trail and Charcoal Wally, but he did finish in front of Berlin, for whom the ground was unsuitable.

David Elsworth decided that the time had come to try Desert Orchid over a longer distance, and on 25 March he was entered in the 2½-mile British Aerospace Novice Chase at Sandown. He started favourite at 11-10 on, and in good ground made nearly all of the running. But he was joined at the last by Clara Mountain, whose jockey, Hywel Davies, proceeded to demonstrate why he is known as one of the best finishers in the business, powering ahead to win by 1½ lengths. After that race there were some who said that Desert Orchid might be better suited by 2 miles, but the pace had been quick throughout and on the strength of one run it was impossible to conclude that he might not be capable of staying the longer trip.

Desert Orchid's final run of the season was in the Contiboard Novice Handicap Chase at Ascot on 12 April, again over 2½ miles. Starting 5-1 favourite, he set a blinding pace until four out, where he blundered badly. With top weight of 11 stone 7, he was giving 17 pounds or more to the first three, and at this stage in the season he was probably feeling the effects of a strenuous first campaign over fences. His strength was sapped, and he finished fifth and once again questions were asked about his ability to stay 2½ miles. However, David Elsworth had no doubts, and he intended to start proving it the following autumn.

The race was won by Repington, trained by the veteran Captain Neville Crump, and sired, coincidentally, by Grey Mirage. □

Desert Orchid completes his morning ritual in his box before allowing Rodney Boult to tack him up.

King George triumph

PRIOR TO HIS TRIUMPH in the 1986 King George VI Chase Desert Orchid had three races earlier in the season. He had returned from his summer holidays in fine form, and was by now considerably lighter in colour than the iron grey four-year-old who had first run over hurdles four seasons previously. His distinctive character had endeared him to everyone at the Whitsbury stables, and even the tough David Elsworth had grown tremendously fond of him:

'We all get attached to horses—they represent us in our endeavours. They're like people: some are bastards, some are very nice, some are tough, some weak—they're all individuals. But those who are best at it are usually characters as well.

'Desert Orchid is an extraordinary character. He has tremendous presence and determination, and he's so easy to train. A marvellous horse.'

Desert Orchid is ridden out each morning by Rodney Boult, Elsworth's vastly experienced head lad. As he does on the racecourse, the grey likes to be in front, leading the string through the Whitsbury lanes to the gallops. Any horse who tries to pull in front of him is physically persuaded to resume its rightful place. He pulls hard on the gallops too, but Boult is always in control, and Elsworth has been quick to acknowledge his debt to his head lad:

'Rodney Boult has a tremendous understanding and rapport with him. He knows the horse so well, and it's a great help to me to have someone of Rodney's understanding and knowledge of horses, to be able to literally guide me. It makes my job so much easier. He has played a very major part in Desert Orchid's development.'

His first race of the season was at Sandown, a course he seems to thrive on. He carried 10 stone 3 in the

Holsten Export Lager Handicap Chase, and made every yard of the running to win by 4 lengths from The Argonaut and Very Promising. However, he was extremely well handicapped, bearing in mind that Very Promising was conceding a massive 25 pounds in weight, and also that Desert Orchid had beaten David Nicholson's horse easily when they had met over hurdles. But those who doubted his ability to stay 2½ miles now had to eat their words.

At Ascot a fortnight later, in the H & T Walker Goddess Handicap Chase, again over 2½ miles, Desert Orchid carried 11 stone 6, and was giving weight to the three horses who finished in front of him that day— Church Warden, Berlin and Amber Rambler. Simon Sherwood has always said that he believes that horses, like athletes, have the odd inexplicable off-day when there is no reason to believe that they are anything but 100% fit, and perhaps Desert Orchid had just that problem.

Whatever it was, he was back to his best in the Frogmore Handicap Chase, also at Ascot but this time over 2 miles, a month later. The ground was good and the pace quick, and Desert Orchid did not have things his own way. His old rival, Charcoal Wally, disputed the lead with him for most of the race, at one point heading the grey. But Desert Orchid had the character to pull back, and went into a clear lead two out, eventually winning by 12 lengths.

Shortly after this David Elsworth announced that Desert Orchid would run next in the King George VI Chase at Kempton Park on Boxing Day. He now had sufficient confidence in the horse to try him over 3 miles, although many people, Rodney Boult included, doubted he would get the trip with his free, front-running style, and bookmakers offered ante-post odds of

20-1. Elsworth, however, never doubted his charge's ability to stay 3 miles. The only question was, who would ride Desert Orchid if Colin Brown chose Combs Ditch?

Sooner or later in his career every top jockey is faced with having to make the choice between two decent horses in the same race. Get it right, and of course there was no other decision. Get it wrong—well, how could you possibly have been so stupid?

For Colin Brown, the moment of truth came a few hours before the King George VI Chase, one of the season's richest and most prestigious races. David Elsworth's entry in the race was double-barrelled—the proven Combs Ditch, twice second in this race and last year beaten only a neck by Wayward Lad in what was a record time, and the popular Desert Orchid, tackling 3 miles for the first time. Brown had the choice of mounts: Sherwood would ride the one he rejected.

Brown was under a certain amount of pressure to ride Combs Ditch from his owners, the Torys, for whom he had also enjoyed considerable success on another smart chaser, Buckbe. Also, Combs Ditch had been working very well at home, and Desert Orchid, although winning the Frogmore Chase at Ascot a fortnight previously, had been well beaten by a moderate field in the H & T Walker Goddess Chase in mid-November. There were other questions to be asked too. Would Desert Orchid get the trip? Would Combs Ditch, as he usually did, win on his seasonal reappearance! Would the ground come up soft, and if so could Desert Orchid cope with it? Brown announced that he would make no decision until the morning of the race. David Elsworth made no attempt to influence him; nor did Richard Burridge.

'Richard was always very fair. He said he knew it

would be a difficult choice for me, but that whatever happened I would still ride Desert Orchid next time out.'

On the morning of the race Brown was one of the first to arrive at Kempton Park. His mind already half made up, he walked the course. The ground was dead, much softer than Desert Orchid would like, but no problem for Combs Ditch. Logically, there was only one option. Brown would ride Combs Ditch.

'I left the decision as late as possible, and it wasn't easy. The main thing that put me off Desert Orchid was that the ground was very heavy that day. Combs Ditch was beaten a neck in the King George the year before and I thought he would run a big race. I took a percentage decision, and I got it wrong.'

Sherwood, meanwhile, pulled on the blue and grey colours of Richard Burridge and had a brief chat with David Elsworth. The Whitsbury trainer likened the situation to a game of poker: in Combs Ditch he had a steady, reliable hand; in Desert Orchid he held the wild card. He thought that if Desert Orchid got the trip he would win, and he was fairly confident that the grey would get the trip.

'I think Colin's made the wrong decision,' he confided to Sherwood, who had actually been hoping to get the ride on the Nick Gaselee-trained Bolands Cross. That went to Peter Scudamore, and Sherwood set about getting acquainted with Desert Orchid.

'I didn't know a great deal about him, but when I'd seen him he'd always looked a bit fast and furious. I was a little bit apprehensive, thinking he was going to rush off with me.

'He took a bit of a grip going down to the start. David Elsworth said he was inclined to jink to the left when they jumped off, so I made sure there was a horse to the left of me. Then I just let him bowl along in front.'

Brown, meanwhile, was having problems of his own: 'As we jumped off I was screaming at all the other jockeys, "Don't let Desert Orchid go!", because I didn't want to be too far behind, and you have to wait on Combs Ditch.

'But they let him go 15 lengths clear. Possibly if I'd been riding him they wouldn't have let him go so far. Anyway, by the time Combs Ditch jumped out of the gate and jumped the first I knew he wasn't going to be winning anything that day.'

In front, Sherwood was having a dream ride: 'He went a bit fast over the first four fences, then he settled down quite well. He was a super jumper and I thought, "We'll just bowl along in front." Going down the back straight last time round, we had a good old blow, then quickened it up quite a lot. He hit the last fence in the back straight quite hard, but it didn't stop him at all.

'Halfway round the final bend I thought to myself, "We're going to win this if we can just hold on. Don't ask any questions yet." Looking over my shoulder around the final bend, I remember seeing the yellow colours of Forgive 'N' Forget just beginning to come. But I never had to ask anything of him until going to the last, and he won as he liked.'

As Desert Orchid stormed up the run-in to the cheers of the huge crowd, there was the sad sight of Combs Ditch, obviously distressed, being pulled up by Colin Brown two out. Forgive 'N' Forget, the 2-1 favourite, faded to fourth, beaten also by Door Latch and Bolands Cross.

Afterwards, Forgive 'N' Forget's trainer, Jimmy Fitzgerald, said that his horse and rider had given Desert Orchid more freedom than they would have done if they'd known him, and none of the other jockeys in the race had expected the grey to get the trip. But that was taking nothing away from Desert Orchid's performance. He had slaughtered a top-quality field by 15 lengths, and Simon Sherwood was delighted:

'It was a great thrill, and it's even more exciting when you win on something that isn't particularly fancied. He gave me the most incredible ride. At the second last they got to within 4 lengths of me, and he did one of his great long jumps and made 4 lengths on Forgive 'N' Forget— and that decided it.'

Colin Brown was gracious in defeat, happy to talk to the press and television journalists, admitting he'd made the wrong decision and offering no excuses. He was, he said, delighted for Desert Orchid and his connections. He meant it.

As Brown drove home quietly in the gathering dusk, reflecting ruefully that racing can be a cruel game, Sherwood went off to celebrate. A chance ride on a 16-1 outsider, uncertain to get the trip in the heavy ground, had turned into the sort of race most jockeys can only dream about. Although he did not know it at the time, it had been a brief but tantalising taste of things to come.

As Richard Burridge had promised him, Colin Brown was back in the saddle for Desert Orchid's next race, the Gainsborough Handicap Chase at Sandown on 7 February. Not that Brown had ever doubted Burridge's word.

'Richard Burridge is one of the most loyal owners I've ever ridden for. After Simon won the King George, the first thing Richard said to me was "You ride him next time." A lot of people would probably have jocked me off at that stage. I was delighted for the connections that he won the King George, even though I wasn't riding him.'

In the Gainsborough, also over 3 miles, Desert Orchid

'On the run-in I remember thinking "get your head down and keep pushing", although I could tell by the reaction of the crowd that I'd won it.'

carried 11 stone 10 and was conceding weight all round. After seeing what had happened in the King George, the other jockeys this time attempted to stay in closer touch with the flying grey—to no avail. He made all, coming home by 10 lengths from Stearsby, Bolands Cross and Catch Phrase. It proved that Kempton had been no fluke, and it took his winnings from first-prize money to over £100,000.

Desert Orchid was now being aimed at the Queen Mother Champion Chase at the Cheltenham Festival meeting in March, but first he went to Wincanton on 26 February for the Jim Ford Challenge Cup. He skated up by 12 lengths in ground that was good to soft, beating Mr Moonraker, Fire Drill and West Tip, winner of the Grand National ten months previously, in what Colin Brown described as 'a really top-class display of jumping'.

After six previous runs in the season, Desert Orchid was still a relatively fresh horse when he went to Cheltenham. Reverting to 2 miles, he showed his old tendency to jump right-handed, losing ground, but he lost nothing in defeat to Pearlyman—arguably the best 2-miler in the country at the time, and Very Promising. The distance between the three of them was only just over 3 lengths, and Desert Orchid certainly made up ground on the run-in. For David Elsworth, it was proof once again that the grey is better suited to a right-handed track:

'The horse certainly doesn't act as well left-handed as he does right-handed. Now why that is I wouldn't know, because he's a beautifully balanced horse and he's a great jumper, and he knows geographically where he's going at Cheltenham. But when they go left-handed he doesn't quicken. You've got a job to see any difference visually, but he doesn't seem to compete as well.

'When he ran in the Champion Chase he was 10 or 15 lengths clear at the fourth last on the far side, but as soon as they started to go left they all came up behind him on the bridle, and up the run-in he started to go on again. So I don't care what they say—he is not as good going left-handed.'

Brown, too, was philosophical: 'It was a good run. Pearlyman was a hard horse to beat that day, and Desert Orchid ran a great race.'

Three weeks later, at Ascot, Desert Orchid ran an even greater race. At 12 stone 4, he was conceding a massive 29 pounds in the Peregrine Handicap Chase, yet he beat Fred Winter's 33-1 outsider, Gold Bearer, ridden by the great Scudamore, despite being headed four out. It was a tremendous display of courageous running, which left even his jockey in awe of the horse's guts:

'He jumped like a stag, but he made a mistake four out. The other horse came by, and I think most people thought, "Oh well, a lot of weight, end of the season, he's beat." But we got into the straight, and I remember there was a strongish headwind, and I just sat behind Scu, and crept up his inside going to the last and took it up. Both horses jumped the last quite slowly because they were knackered, and we won by two lengths. That was a great, great performance—one of the best I remember.'

It was even more remarkable if you consider that Gold Bearer was 19 pounds out of the handicap.

Elsworth had one more ambitious target at the end of a hard season—the prestigious Whitbread Gold Cup. At 3 miles 5 furlongs, it was the longest distance Desert Orchid had ever attempted, and he was also suffering from corns, which necessitated removing them and packing the horse's feet with ice the night before the race. But with the ground drying up to firm at this stage of the season, it was too much even for this courageous animal. Early in the race, Brown knew that the writing was on the wall:

'By the time I jumped the second, I knew that in an ideal world I'd pull him up. But I went round a circuit, jumped the water in the back straight and pulled him up then.'

After a hard season, and with the additional problem of corns, it had perhaps been one race too many. The race was won by another flamboyant front runner, Lean Ar Aghaidh (pronounced Lan Ar-wye), ridden by the young jockey, Guy Landau, who had produced such a bold display of jumping in the Grand National three weeks earlier.

Desert Orchid went off for his summer break, first to the fields of Jimmy Burridge's Leicestershire estate, then to his son's home on the North Yorkshire moors, where he would spend time walking and trotting on the lonely roads to help strengthen his legs for the next campaign. Jackie Parrish was married now, and the combination of a stable lad's unsociable hours and relatively low pay hastened her decision, albeit a reluctant one, to leave racing. Her place as Desert Orchid's 'lass' was taken by the elfin-faced Janice Coyle.

And another key figure in this great team was also considering his future. Colin Brown was 32 now, and not many jump jockeys go on much beyond that age. The falls get harder, the recovery time longer. He had a young family to consider, and he had bought a pub, the Ibex in Chaddleworth near Hungerford, which he was busy developing into one of the most convivial pubs in the area. Despite the attraction of riding the country's greatest chaser, the next season was to be his last. □

Brown's farewell

THE 1987/88 NATIONAL HUNT season was Desert Orchid's sixth in succession, and, remarkably, he had never in that time been off the racecourse through injury. He has always been a very strong, sound horse, unlike so many jumpers who sometimes have to miss a whole season while leg trouble clears up.

His seasonal reappearance this time was in the Terry Biddlecombe Challenge Trophy at Wincanton on 29 October. Starting 7-1 on favourite, he won this three-horse race by a distance, and Colin Brown really just had to sit on him.

'He skated up! Jumped like a stag, ears pricked all the way round. He really showed off over the last two—stood off a mile!'

David Elsworth really wanted to put a good race into the horse next time out, but the Rank Boxing Day Trial Chase at Kempton on 18 November, over 2½ miles, seemed framed for him. Once again he won as he pleased, beating Bishops Yarn by 12 lengths, with Galway Blaze back in third place. Colin Brown rode a double that day, when Sir Blake made his successful debut over hurdles.

Desert Orchid did not have things all his own way next time out, in the Tingle Creek Handicap Chase at Sandown on 5 December. He was giving away 2 stone to David Nicholson's progressive young chaser Long Engagement, and although he either led or disputed the lead throughout, the weight told two fences from home, and he went down by 3 lengths. But he lost nothing in defeat here, and in fact it was a good preparation race for the King George.

Twelve months previously Desert Orchid had come to Kempton on Boxing Day as a 20-1 outsider in the King George. No one, David Elsworth apart, had believed he was the type of horse to stay 3 miles. Now,

Clearing the water jump in the Terry Biddlecombe Challenge Trophy at Wincanton on 29 October 1987. *Colin Brown:* 'He was showing off that day. He went all the way round with his ears pricked. It was a great feeling, because when I was out in the country I just left him to it and he did the job nicely.

'Second time round I remember going to the first fence down the back and he spooked for some reason, hit the top and I thought "we're gone!", but he got it all together as we landed. He really showed off over the last two fences and you could tell he was loving it!

'The only trouble was that there was nothing good enough to give him a bit of a race.'

however, he was evens favourite. The only worry was that with two other confirmed front-runners, Beau Ranger and Cybrandian, in the race, these three might cut each other's throats in a battle for the lead.

Which is exactly what happened. Right from the start all three set a suicidal pace, and it was obvious that they would run themselves into the ground well before the end. David Elsworth knew that Martin Pipe would instruct Beau Ranger's jockey, Peter Scudamore, to take on Desert Orchid, and he told Colin Brown not to be intimidated.

'David said, "You go out and make it: he likes to be out in front." So I hopped out the gate and we went a 5-furlong sprint pace over the first four or five fences. And I remember thinking, "Well, I'll sit and Scu will take a pull," but no, he never did, and he probably sat and thought, "Well, I'll get back in front." It was stupid really—we shouldn't have done that.'

The third of this fiercely galloping trio, Cybrandian,

Desert Orchid leads over the first in the Rank Boxing Day Trial Chase at Kempton on 18 November 1987. He won by 12 lengths from Bishops Yarn and Galway Blaze, the only other runners.

ridden by Ronnie Beggan, fell at the fourteenth, and shortly after that Beau Ranger had had enough, and faded to finish an eventual fourth. Desert Orchid, as brave as ever, was still in front on the final bend, but it was really only that searing early pace that had put him there. Behind him, the challenge was unfolding from the French horse, Nupsala, and Jimmy Fitzgerald's Forgive 'N' Forget, ridden by Mark Dwyer.

Despite being one of the best chasers in France, winning two of his previous five outings, Nupsala was ignored in the betting and started at 25-1. But his jockey, André Pommier, had him well poised as they entered the straight for the final time, and although Forgive 'N' Forget crashed heavily at the last, it is doubtful that he would have been in a position to mount a serious challenge on the Frenchman. Desert Orchid, for his part, finished 15-length second, worn out by the early

Colin Brown: 'It was one of those races that was really framed for him, but there wasn't much opposition, especially as Bishops Yarn is always held up. He needed a good race here, but he didn't have one really.' [*Simon Sherwood, riding Galway Blaze:* 'Richard Guest and I accepted that Colin was going to go and win it, so we just went round and did our own thing']

battle. With hindsight Brown, who concedes that by this stage in his career Desert Orchid did not need to make every yard of the running, says that he should probably have used different tactics, although he was, as ever, generous in defeat.

'Nupsala came there like a good horse, although he's never quite shown that form since. But the form on the day was good really.'

It had been a hard race, and Desert Orchid was given a rest until 6 February, when he went to Sandown for the Gainsborough Chase, again over 3 miles. Carrying 12 stone, he was giving over a stone in weight all round, including a massive 17 pounds to Charter Party, and 21 pounds to Rhyme 'N' Reason, another Elsworth-trained horse.

In soft ground, he was beaten by both of them, although he led until two out. Charter Party won by 8

Colin Brown: 'He did nothing wrong that day. He gave Long Engagement lumps of weight, and we were beaten three lengths. We weren't disappointed, because Long Engagement ended up having a very good season.'

lengths, and Rhyme 'N' Reason got up in the final strides to snatch second place. Five weeks later Charter Party won the Gold Cup by 6 lengths, and Rhyme 'N' Reason lifted the Grand National in April, so, looking at it objectively, Desert Orchid performed pretty well at Sandown that day. However, Colin Brown recalls that Elsworth was somewhat worried about the horse:

'David didn't think the horse was quite right round about that time, but I came back and said I thought he was just coming back well. And that was a great race as it turned out, when you consider how the other two went on to peform—a very, very good race. It was a great performance, and I was really pleased with him.'

Desert Orchid was being aimed at the Queen Mother Champion Chase at Cheltenham, but first he went to Wincanton on 25 February to contest the Jim Ford Challenge Cup. This three-horse race saw the reappearance, after a long layoff, of the popular Burrough Hill Lad, but it was the third horse, Kildimo, that upset Colin Brown's plans that day.

'Kildimo had been a bit in and out, but it was going to be difficult to judge what sort of pace to ride the race. I set off at a decent sort of pace, and he jumped like a stag. Down the back I really quickened, and I could hear Kildimo not very far off me, but I reckoned I had enough left in the tank to quicken up.

'I jumped the last ditch on the far side, and he stood off a mile and really flew it. I changed my hands to quicken up, and he flew the cross-fence, and I couldn't believe it because as I turned into the straight Kildimo was still two lengths behind me! I came over the last two and rallied, and Kildimo came at the last, and we asked for a really big one, and got it, and Kildimo still stuck in there and bloody well beat me!

'I said to David and Richard, "Maybe I've ridden the

74

wrong race. Maybe I should have jumped off and gone like the clappers, or perhaps waited and let Kildimo get in front a bit soon." But they both thought I'd ridden it all right—we were just beaten on the day.'

The distance was 1½ lengths, and perhaps it was another case of Desert Orchid not being at his tip-top best on the day. Kildimo is a very good chaser, but he is inconsistent, and has never won another race since.

The result did not affect David Elsworth's plans to run Desert Orchid in the Queen Mother Champion Chase on the second day of the Cheltenham Festival meeting. Nor did it affect Colin Brown's plans. He had decided back in January that this was to be his final season. The Ibex was thriving, and he was in the process of taking over another pub, the Wheatsheaf at Chilton Foliat. After 292 winners, and a distinguished career with Desert Orchid, Brown could retire with honour and no regrets.

'I wasn't tempted to carry on because of Desert Orchid, because you never know what might happen. He might have broken down, or something else might have gone wrong. You can't carry on just because of one good horse.'

It was a sensible, level-headed decision, taken at the right time.

Brown rode Sir Blake in the opening race of the second day, the Sun Alliance Novice Hurdle. He was in fourth place when he fell at the last, and Brown is convinced he would have won. Subsequently, under Brendan Powell, Sir Blake put up some stunning performances as a novice chaser, before tragically breaking a leg on the gallops. It is this sort of mortality, unexpected and unaccountable, that throws such a favourable light on Desert Orchid's performances over the years.

In the Queen Mother Champion Chase Desert Orchid faced some very tough opposition. Pearlyman, the previous year's winner, once again lined up against him, as did Very Promising, Panto Prince, Long Engagement and Josh Gifford's highly rated chaser, Midnight Count. Despite the soft ground the time was quick, and Pearlyman again demonstrated his superiority in this event, beating Desert Orchid by 5 lengths, with Very Promising back in third. Brown was frustrated not to win on Desert Orchid for the final time, but happy enough with the way he ran.

'That was a good run. He jumped slightly to the right, the way he always did, but it was satisfactory.'

Brown rode one more race, on Calapaez in the *Daily Express* Triumph Hurdle, for Brooke Saunders. They finished tenth. Then he told David Elsworth of his decision to retire.

Colin Brown had ridden 43 races on Desert Orchid, and won 17 of them. It is difficult to imagine a better record. ☐

Colin Brown hard at work on the run in.

Simon Sherwood

W HEN COLIN BROWN retired after the 1988 Cheltenham Festival meeting, the Burridges were anxious to replace him on Desert Orchid with a jockey who would be available to ride the horse every time he ran. For this reason Peter Scudamore, with his commitment to both Charlie Brooks and Martin Pipe, was discounted, and, while other jockeys were considered, it was inevitable that in the end the ride would go to Simon Sherwood.

For many people, Sherwood was the best jockey of his time. Twice amateur champion, he had given Scudamore a tremendous run for his money in his first season as a professional, finishing only eleven winners behind him at the end of the 1985/86 season. His style was smooth and sympathetic: he never hit a horse unnecessarily. An articulate and intelligent man, he could read a race well, and, most important on a front-runner like Desert Orchid, he was an excellent judge of pace. While Scudamore is capable of riding the most storming finish, and you can really see him at work on the horse, Sherwood was just as good. He simply did it in a quieter style.

Three weeks after the Queen Mother Champion Chase, Desert Orchid went to Liverpool to contest the Chivas Regal Cup, over 3 miles 1 furlong. The ground was good, but three things worried Sherwood—the tight bends of the Mildmay course at Aintree, the fact that it is left-handed, and the presence in the field of Beau Ranger, another confirmed front-runner.

'I knew Beau Ranger would take us on, and I didn't want a repeat of last season's King George, when they cut each other's throats by setting such a suicidal pace early on.'

It was to Sherwood's immense relief then, although wretched luck for Beau Ranger's connections, when the

Desert Orchid and Simon Sherwood on their way to victory in the 1988 Whitbread Gold Cup. The grey made most of the running, although Run and Skip led briefly down the back straight second time round. 'We were only overtaken for a short time going off the bottom bend, but it was a blessing in disguise because it gave him a chance to have a blow. He won a couple of lengths, but he won quite nicely.'

horse spread a plate as the field circled at the start and had to be withdrawn. After that there were no problems whatsoever: the left-handed bogey was laid to rest at last, and Sherwood was delighted with Desert Orchid's performance as the horse beat Kildimo by 8 lengths.

'He gave me a super ride, although he was a little bit sticky at his fences. We literally only hunted round the first circuit, and going down the back straight for the last time I gave him a slap down the shoulder, and he started to perform at his fences and jump them properly. He won easily, going away. My saddle slipped jumping the last so I had to sit quietly on him on the run-in, but he was never under pressure.'

After such an easy run at Liverpool, Desert Orchid was in prime form for the Whitbread Gold Cup at Sandown Park a fortnight later. Because of a slight worry about his corns, which had caused him to pull up in the race twelve months earlier, he was led round on the grass, but anxiety proved unwarranted. The grey made all, apart from a short stretch by the railway fences, when he had a good blow and Run and Skip took it up for a bit. In the end he beat Kildimo by 2½ lengths, with Strands of Gold third. The favourite, Aquilifer, ridden by the late Paul Croucher, was totally unsuited by the fast ground, and his challenge faded three out. Sherwood returned to the winner's enclosure with a broad smile on his face.

'He jumped fantastically that day, and he loved the good ground. Kildimo came upsides me between the second last and the last, but even then I knew I had a bit to spare. He quickened up the hill and won very nicely.'

If anyone still had any doubts about Desert Orchid being the public's favourite racehorse, they would have had to concede on that day that they were wrong. The huge roar from the crowd as he jumped the last simply increased in volume on the run-in and reached a crescendo as he passed the winning post: all the jockeys riding in the race said afterwards that they had never heard a roar like it before. There was a stampede from the stands to the winner's enclosure, more cheers, and quite a few tears too. Quite simply, Desert Orchid had captured the public's imagination in the way that few horses ever do.

And that was it for the season. Desert Orchid had run nine races, won four of them, been second in four others and third once. He retired to Jimmy Burridge's Leicestershire farm for his summer break. The best was still to come.

For the 1988/89 season, David Elsworth followed his now familiar pattern of preparing Desert Orchid for his first major target of the season, the King George. There would be a prep race at Wincanton in October, another run in early December, then straight to Kempton Park on Boxing Day. Depending on the weather, the ground and the horse's well-being, owners and trainer would then consider the Gold Cup, and the Whitbread.

Desert Orchid likes Wincanton, a good, fast, right-handed galloping track. Apart from being unplaced there in his second ever race in 1983, he has never been beaten at the Somerset course, and the 1988 Terry Biddlecombe Challenge Trophy was no exception. The grey won by 15 lengths, and Sherwood never had to move a muscle on him.

'He was simply showing off to the crowd that day. From the third last all the way up to the winning post they were standing three or four deep, and I swear he was playing to the gallery. He was more concerned about looking photogenic than he was about jumping his fences properly!'

On 2 December Desert Orchid put up another display

of immaculate jumping at Sandown, to beat Jim Thorpe and Panto Prince 15 lengths in the Tingle Creek Handicap Chase. By the time he jumped the Pond fence, there was no doubt about the result. Simon Sherwood's record on the horse was now five races, five wins.

Twenty-four hours before the King George, Richard Burridge went to extraordinary lengths to ensure that Desert Orchid was not 'got at' prior to the big race. After Christmas lunch at his Yorkshire home, he drove down to David Elsworth's Hampshire yard, where he spent the night in his car just a few yards from the horse's box. Aware of doping rumours which had been circulating, and perhaps mindful of the mysterious flop of the favourite, Playschool, in the Gold Cup in March, Burridge was taking no chances.

With the official going good to firm, Desert Orchid started at 2-1 on. As usual, he jumped off in front, and with both Kildimo and Vodkatini taking him on, the five-horse field set a cracking pace which at one stage had Sherwood a bit worried:

'He was buzzing a bit too much over the first mile, and I wasn't able to give him a breather in the final turn. Vodkatini came upsides me at the third last—he was quicker at the fences but then he's a 2-miler and Desert Orchid is a 3-miler. We were only a length and a half ahead of Kildimo at the last fence, but I just pressed the button and rode him hands and heels.'

The eventual winning distance was 4 lengths, with Vodkatini third, and once again the grey came home to a massive roar from the huge crowd, Colin Brown among them. After the race John Francome, commentating on Channel 4, summed it up by saying that Desert Orchid did more work on the gallops at home than he did at Kempton Park that day. Sherwood, remarking that he thought that Desert Orchid had got

Chivas Regal Chase, Aintree, 7 April 1988. Desert Orchid clears the water jump on his way to winning for the first time on a left-handed track.

into the habit of slightly playing with Kildimo when they raced against each other, was convinced that the horse should now be aimed for the Gold Cup. Richard Burridge was more cautious, saying that it would depend on the state of the ground, while David Elsworth said that no decision would be made until after the middle of February: Desert Orchid's immediate aim was the Victor Chandler Chase at Ascot in three weeks' time.

Simon Sherwood did not enjoy the Victor Chandler. Desert Orchid was giving Panto Prince 22 pounds, and his three other rivals—Ida's Delight, Long Engagement and Vodkatini—even more weight. He was also reverting to 2 miles.

'It was a hard race. I think Brendan [Powell] decided that he was going to hassle us the whole way on Panto Prince and go upsides right from the start. We went off very fast. Desert Orchid knew it was 2 miles because of the quicker pace, and he knew Panto Prince was taking him on, and he did some stupid jumps, taking off too far away from the fences.

'That was the least enjoyable ride I had on him: we were being harassed the whole way round. He pecked on landing at the last ditch and we very nearly came down, but he found a fifth leg.

'As we came into the straight, there was Long Engagement, Panto Prince and Desert Orchid all upsides. Brendan had the inside and had gained a couple of lengths from us on the bottom bend. We were almost upsides him at the second last, but he was quicker away from the fence and suddenly we were a couple of lengths down. At the last we were almost upsides again—we jumped it together but again Panto was quicker away from it.'

By now the crowd, revelling in one of the most memorable finishes Ascot has ever seen, were getting behind their hero with a huge roar. Even David Elsworth thought he was beaten, but Sherwood had other ideas as the two horses strove for the line:

'We then had to dig really deep. I had to hit him for the first time—a couple of times going to the last and two or three on the run-in. In a situation like that it helps you get a bit more rhythm. In the last 50 yards he started to lean on Panto and I had to straighten him out, but we just got up.'

The official distance was a head. Afterwards, David Elsworth admitted: 'That's the hardest race he's had so far. Three times I thought he was beaten.'

And Sherwood, his empathy with Desert Orchid now developed to a degree seldom reached between man and horse, later remarked, 'On the run-in he had his ears right back, really trying. But as soon as we passed the post and I dropped my hands he put his head up and pricked his ears, thinking, "That's it: another scalp!"'

In the Gainsborough Chase at Sandown on 4 February, Desert Orchid once again took on his old rival Kildimo, as well as Charter Party and Pegwell Bay, and it was the winner of that season's Mackeson Gold Cup and A. F. Budge Trophy, both at Cheltenham, that posed the biggest threat. Not that Sherwood was very concerned:

'I had one of the nicest rides I ever had on him that day. Pegwell Bay is obviously a very good horse and we had to give him a stone and a half, which is a lot to have to give a Mackeson winner, and he'd won those races well.

'It was the usual form. We made all on the first circuit, then Pegwell Bay came past me going into the back straight for the last time. Desert Orchid accepted this and was happy to settle in behind, and he had a nice old blow down the back. At the railway fences Pegwell Bay was jumping a bit left and I was a bit worried that he might tip up and bring us down, so I jumped out a little bit wider just to avoid that possibility.

'Then I just sat on him. We went upsides going to the Pond fence, and he put in a very good jump at the last to go half a length clear. Pegwell Bay was a little slow getting into his stride, and I just had to do hands and heels. We won by a length easily, and he was going away. That was certainly one of his most impressive runs.'

As has become the custom at Sandown, the roar of the crowd as Desert Orchid came up the hill threatened to lift the roof of the stand off. He was given three cheers as he entered the winner's enclosure, and the official who called "horses away" was heartily booed. Every other jockey present that day stood on the weighing-room steps to clap him in. It was an unprecedented display of affection for a horse who had become a hero, an affection which extends far beyond the realms of racing itself.

Three weeks later it was confirmed that Desert Orchid would go for the Gold Cup. ☐

Colin Brown, who always tries to be present when Desert Orchid runs, joins the Burridges and Janice Coyle after the 1988 King George.

86

The Cheltenham Gold Cup

I wasn't too concerned. It was rather unfortunate that the weather was so unpleasant, but I didn't think it would be any disadvantage to Desert Orchid, because he's a very good jumper, a good mover; and I thought he was better equipped to deal with the ground than anything else in the race.—**David Elsworth**

THERE IS SOMETHING ABOUT the Cheltenham Gold Cup that sets it on a higher plateau than any other steeplechase—the Grand National included. For a horse it is a test of stamina; of the ability to jump those difficult fences to perfection and still get away quick enough to keep a field of top-class rivals at bay; of the guts to keep going—after 3½ miles—up that awesome hill to the line. For a jockey it is the ultimate test of horsemanship, skill, patience, timing and the ability to ride a finish.

This is not to take anything away from the Grand National—perhaps the most famous race in the world—but it's fair to say that the National is something of a lottery, made so by the combination of horses which are not even good enough to get in the handicap jumping huge fences, which many of the horses have never seen before. There is no lottery about the Gold Cup. The fences are genuine, the horses top-class. Ask some of the hard men of bygone days, like David Nicholson and Jeff King, and they will tell you that as both jockey and trainer the Gold Cup is Blue Riband. Ask Richard Dunwoody, the only contemporary jockey to have won both, and he will tell you the same thing.

The weather on Gold Cup day often throws up something unexpected. In 1987 a snowstorm delayed the start of the race by over an hour. In 1989 snow once again played a major role, although this time it was overnight.

Every Festival-goer staying in the Cotswolds on the night prior to the Gold Cup awoke that morning to the sight of a healthy blizzard raging. On the high hills overlooking the racecourse the snow was up to three inches deep. In the amphitheatre of the racecourse itself, the problem was water, and plenty of it. At 11 am the fire brigade's pumps were in action by the second last fences on the chase course, and the stewards were sufficiently concerned to call for a noon inspection. Perhaps at any other meeting, on any other day, they would have called it off. But this was Gold Cup day, with so many other factors to consider. And there is nothing to stop connections from withdrawing a horse on the morning of a race.

Richard Burridge is a sensitive man, more concerned about the well-being of his beloved horse than he is about the prizes that Desert Orchid might net him. From early that morning he faced an agonising decision about whether or not to run the grey. He was acutely aware that the horse would hate the ground, and he also knew how much the public loved his charge: he said later that, had he withdrawn, he would have asked for ten minutes' start in the car before the announcement was made on the public address system!

Burridge faced a very logical argument from David Elsworth, who was not having an easy time of things either.

'When I got there,' explained Elsworth, 'I didn't get any help from the press and TV people who were making a great drama of it, saying, "is he going to run?" I said, "of course he's going to run!" But Richard

Burridge was apprehensive, because he felt the ground would be a disadvantage and he had reservations about it, with all the pressure from the media it was making my life, and his decision, even more difficult. We knew the horse loved good ground and could run off it—so can most horses. Nobody likes wet ground, but some can cope with it better than others, and I thought he was better equipped to deal with it than the others because he's such a well-balanced horse who jumps with great precision and accuracy and who has tremendous confidence in himself. And he was going to be in front anyway.

'I would not jeopardise his wellbeing. Remember that I took him out at Kempton in October because the ground was too *firm*. I regard firm ground as more of a threat than soft ground, because it's far easier to mess up a horse on firm ground than on soft.

'Anyway, I won the day, and what a bloody good job I did. We would have deprived racing of a great day if he hadn't run.'

Perhaps it was Simon Sherwood, keen to go for Gold ever since Desert Orchid's triumph in the Gainsborough at Sandown, who finally persuaded Burridge to run. Sherwood rode the first and reported that although it was wet and sloppy, the horses were going through the ground. He also promised that if Desert Orchid was unhappy, he would pull him up after two fences. Burridge agreed. They would go for it.

Just before 3.30 pm the runners were circling at the start. The rain had stopped, but the ground was still heavy, ideal for the Irish challenger Carvills Hill, and for the John Edwards trained Yahoo, quoted in the morning papers at 40-1 and the subject of some hefty wagers as a result. There was a lot of money too, for Fulke Walwyn's smart chaser Ten Plus.

There is a buzz that goes round Cheltenham just before the start of the Gold Cup that can be likened to the buzz of an audience prior to the opening night of a great theatrical event. It begins with the anticipatory chatter, a chatter that subsides as the lights dim—'they're under starter's orders'—then the stage lights go up—'they're off'—and suddenly the play's the thing, there's no going back now, we settle down to watch the drama unfold.

Simon Sherwood jumped Desert Orchid off in front and settled him quickly. As the field passed the stands for the first time he was closely tracked by Ten Plus, Yahoo and Charter Party. Carvills Hill, as planned, was held up towards the rear in the early stages, as was The Thinker. The first drama came at the sixth fence when Golden Freeze went down, and one fence later Irish hopes were dashed when Carvills Hill hit the deck. The Thinker, winner in 1987, went at the 10th, and now Richard Dunwoody on Charter Party was pressing Desert Orchid up front, with Ten Plus and Yahoo still in close attendance.

At the 14th Ten Plus moved into the lead, and headed Desert Orchid by two lengths, running comfortably. But tragedy struck three out, the notorious downhill fence, when Ten Plus went down and broke a leg. For Simon Sherwood, unaware at that stage of the gravity of the fall, it was a momentary fillip in what was turning out to be a very, very hard race.

'I was worried about Ten Plus before the start, but when he sadly went down I thought, "We've got this won."

'I could not believe it when Yahoo appeared upsides us! I thought "We're beat, we're stuffed now, no way are we going to win this." Yahoo went on and I thought "I'm going to be second again in the Gold Cup—sod it!"

'But at the second last he didn't get any further away, and there was a patch about ten strides from the last fence when Desert Orchid suddenly quickened for three or four strides. From being a length-and-a-half down we were half-a-length down. Going to the last I thought "God, we're wrong!", and I totally left him to it and he just popped over it.'

By now most of the 55,000 crowd, personal finances forgotten, were making one final, roof-raising effort on behalf of the grey horse as he fought his way home. And Simon Sherwood was getting down to work.

'I thought to myself "This is the Gold Cup. Give it everything you've got. Keep your head down and keep kicking."'

'Suddenly we started to get into another gear. He started to run. He began to run in towards Yahoo and I had to correct him, but by then he was going away. We went a length clear, and I remember just jumping up in my saddle.'

David Elsworth, watching from the stands, and well aware of Desert Orchid's dislike for left-handed tracks, had also, for a short time, been a worried man.

'When Ten Plus went down Yahoo was left on the inner and as they went round the elbow we looked to be in trouble, but I thought, "When we straighten up we'll beat him." But then I began to get very worried. Going to the last I thought "We'll pick him up now," but he didn't, and I thought, "We're going to be pushed to win this."'

'I was surprised that he took so long to beat Yahoo: it took him an awful long time to do it. But having said that, Simon Sherwood was a very sympathetic jockey, and the horse just popped the last and then got the better of his rival.'

Like Jonjo O'Neill on Dawn Run three years

previously, Sherwood punched the air in triumph as Desert Orchid crossed the line, followed home by Yahoo, Charter Party and Bonanza Boy. As the jockeys pulled their horses up and turned to come back in, Tom Morgan, Richard Dunwoody and Peter Scudamore all came across to Sherwood to shake him warmly, and at length, by the hand. It was an outstanding display of the camaraderie of jump racing.

'All three came across with great big smiles on their

faces,' said Sherwood. 'It was a mark of their respect for the horse. Everyone was thrilled. I even saw Martin Pipe clapping us in.'

The winner's enclosure was bedlam as journalists, photographers and officials fought for space, and the crowd did the same on the surrounding terraces as the presentations were made. Janice Coyle and the Burridges could not hide their emotions and their delight, and the Queen Mother came to pay her respects to a horse who, hating every inch of the going, had produced a staggering display of raw courage and sheer, bloody-minded, determination. Sherwood remarked later that when Yahoo took over at the second last, every other horse bar Desert Orchid would have thrown in the towel.

'Desert Orchid wouldn't know when to give up. From a jockey's point of view he's the perfect horse to ride. He's so good at his obstacles. He lobs along and paces himself. Come the end of the race, so long as he's still on the bridle, you know you've got a bit more speed than anything else.'

For Fulke Walwyn, who earlier in the day had unveiled the statue of the great five-times Gold Cup winner Golden Miller, the death of Ten Plus was a tragedy; and as the celebrations went on around Desert Orchid, Kevin Mooney, just yards away, was plumbing the depths of despair. Jump racing is about agony as well as ecstasy, like different sides of the same coin. One face of it may be ugly, but you cannot separate the two.

But, at the end of the day, jump racing is about winning. David Elsworth's determination and faith in running Desert Orchid had been vindicated. So, too, had been the conviction of Simon Sherwood, who went home to Lambourn for a quiet dinner with family and friends. The adrenalin was still pumping: it would take a day or two to sink in. The Burridges celebrated, also quietly, at their Cotswolds hotel, the Gold Cup in the centre of the table. And the crowds went home happy, at the end of another three matchless March days, with only one subject on their lips.

It had been one of those great sporting occasions when, in years to come, it will be good to be able to say, 'I was there!' □

QUEEN MOTHER CHAMPION CHASE 1988
Desert Orchid, with the Burridges following, is led in by Janice Coyle, having
finished second to Pearlyman. This was the very last time Colin Brown sat on him.
'I hadn't actually announced my retirement then—only my wife Annie and David
Elsworth knew. I would have finished that day if I'd won, but I'd taken the ride on
Calapaez for Brooke Saunders the next day—Simon stuck me in for it—and I didn't
want to let her down.'

ASCOT—VICTOR CHANDLER CHASE—14 JANUARY 1989
Simon Sherwood: 'This is a rather elegant picture of Desert Orchid in the parade.
Rather elegant of the jockey too, if I may say so!'

'Brendan Powell maintained that Panto Prince wasn't firing properly when Desert Orchid had beaten him in the Tingle Creek Chase at Sandown a month earlier. But they were much more confident this time and they had decided on different tactics: they were going to hassle us right from the start, which over 2 miles is a very good ploy, because you can't really settle him.

'He went clear of me coming into the straight, and I knew it was going to be a right old slog, but Desert Orchid had the guts for it. He wasn't going to give up for one second.

'As a jockey, you can nearly always sense straight away if you've got the race or not, and I remember thinking as we crossed the line "yes!", and shouting across to Brendan "what do you reckon?", and he said "yes, well done you bugger!" As I came into the winner's enclosure David Elsworth said "Don't you think we should hover?", but I said "no—we've won".

'And we had.'

Janice Coyle cleaning out Desert Orchid's box at Whitsbury.
The glamour of leading jump racing's best loved horse
around the parade rings of Cheltenham and Sandown is
tempered with the fact that, day in, day out, he has to be
looked after at home.

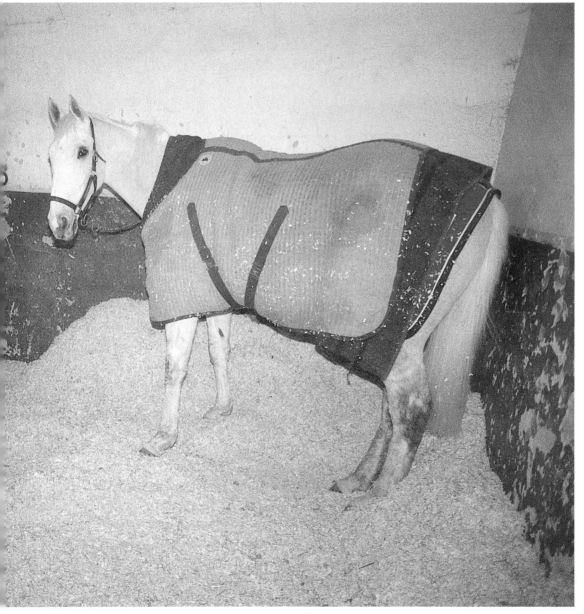

Desert Orchid leads
Kildimo over the
Pond fence in the
1988 Whitbread
Gold Cup.

Desert Orchid and Pegwell Bay on the run-in in the Gainsborough. It wasn't as close as many people thought: Simon Sherwood was always confident and said afterwards that Desert Orchid won 'cosily'.

CHELTENHAM GOLD CUP 1989
The strain shows on Simon Sherwood's face as he and Desert Orchid fight their way up the run in, having jumped the last.
'I can remember, having jumped the last, thinking "God I'm tired!" But the thought flashed through my mind, "remember, it's the Gold Cup, it's the Gold Cup", and somehow you just go through the pain barrier and you find renewed strength.'

CHELTENHAM GOLD CUP 1989—

Simon Sherwood:

'He got quite a loud ovation as he cantered down to the start. That's something that has caught on for his last three or four races: I think it started at Sandown.

'He's a bit of a show-off! He pricks his ears up and takes a right good grip and looks up at the crowd, very much aware of what's going on.'

'We were both tired going to the last. We were wrong approaching the fence so I had to drop my hands and let him pop it, but even when he's wrong he's still quite quick through the air, although he takes a while to get into his stride when he's landed.'

'I was worried he would go to the right on the run in, so David Elsworth had said to get him over to the right so that we didn't lose time coming up the hill. As we jumped the last I hit him with my right hand, and he actually went totally the other way!'

'A huge roar went up as we came into the enclosure, and he pricked his ears up. There was a moment as we walked into the enclosure when a whole mass of people came running towards us, and I thought, "Crickey, he's going to go bananas!" But he carried on walking straight as a die, and it didn't bother him at all.'
'It was the most amazing roar, which sadly the television microphones didn't pick up, because they were waterlogged.'

'As I took the saddle off him there was some Irishman standing there—I don't know who the hell he was. Anyway, he came up and kissed me!'

'I think this is the most lovely photograph. It's almost as if Desert Orchid is thinking "Oh! Here's the Queen Mother! Best behaviour!" It looks as though there is a mutual respect between the two of them.'

The finish of the 1989 Cheltenham Gold Cup. Simon Sherwood raises his arm in triumph as Desert Orchid crosses the line in front of Yahoo.

Janice Coyle and Simon Sherwood after
the 1988 Victor Chandler Chase at Ascot—'the
least enjoyable race I ever rode on him'.

Liverpool

AFTER HIS TRIUMPH at Cheltenham, Desert Orchid had become, if such a thing is possible, even more of a people's champion. David Elsworth, well aware of this, felt it was only fair to the public to run him once more before the season's end, but was against the horse defending his Whitbread Gold Cup title, with top weight of 12 stone 2 and the possibility of firm ground. Instead, Desert Orchid was entered for the Martell Cup on the first day of the Aintree meeting.

He was, of course, the centre of attention on that first day. Even BBC television's coverage, normally fairly staid, announced in its opening credits that the racing from Liverpool starred Desert Orchid. It was inevitable, perhaps, that something would go wrong.

Desert Orchid went off the 5-4 favourite. As they jumped out of the gate, he immediately took the lead, tracked closely by Peter Scudamore on Beau Ranger and Richard Dunwoody on Charter Party. However, Simon Sherwood already had cause for slight concern:

'He felt very good in the paddock, but normally when I take him down to the start he tanks off with me, and this time he just took a bit of a hold.

'Down at the start you would have had to be hyper-sensitive to think there was anything different with him, but as soon as we jumped the first he didn't give me a feeling of being wildly happy. I think it was a combination of the ground, which was pretty tacky and nasty, and also the old horse realised straightaway that he was going left-handed again, and it was always going to be a different sort of race to when he was there last time. Beau Ranger was hassling us up the inside, and I was jumping to the right the whole way round.

'After a circuit I hoped we'd be 3 or 4 lengths clear so I could give him a blow, but they were right up his backside the whole way. And every time he jumped he

Martell Cup.
Liverpool, 6 April
1989. Desert Orchid
is ahead of the field
at the water jump on
the first circuit.

went a little bit right and I had to hook him on to the rails again, and the old horse started to say, "I'm not enjoying this very much."'

The field passed the stands and turned into the tight left-handed bend to head out into the country for the second time. As they approached the twelfth fence they were still tightly bunched, Desert Orchid just half a length up on Charter Party. In the next few seconds the whole complexion of the race changed, and a remarkable record came to a sudden and sad end. Desert Orchid brushed the top of the fence, failed to pick his hind legs up, and pitched forward. The unbeaten partnership of nine races was on the floor, and in an entirely separate, unconnected fall, Richard Dunwoody and Charter Party also parted company. Beau Ranger was hampered and Delius was left in front, but at the business end of the race Yahoo avenged his Cheltenham defeat, winning by 10 lengths. It was hard to begrudge John Edwards and Tom Morgan that success.

Both Desert Orchid and Charter Party, and their riders, were, thankfully, unharmed, and many a pair of binoculars in the stands continued to track the riderless grey as he galloped on round. Richard Burridge, trembling with concern, leapt a five-foot railing and was first to reach the horse as he trotted up the run-in. Sherwood walked in, wiping the Aintree mud from his breeches and reflecting on the end of an unbeaten partnership. It was already in the back of his mind that he had probably sat on Desert Orchid for the last time.

'As I went into the fence I thought, "I don't feel particularly happy. We haven't gone a wildly good gallop and I'm going to have to try to quicken it up or they're just going to smother me any moment."

'They quickened up behind me, and he quickened up into it as a result. He was slightly wrong—nine and a half times out of ten he'd have done a little shuffle and got himself right, but this time he didn't. He didn't pick his hind legs up as high as he should have done and he caught them in the fence and pitched forward. I felt that he just accepted his fate.

'It is always in the back of your mind that after a Gold Cup the horse is going to be over the top, and Desert Orchid was over the top at Liverpool. When he made that mistake it was a tired mistake: he wasn't sparking at all.

'Yahoo won it well. Everything was in favour of him winning it—he loved the ground—and everything was against Desert Orchid winning it. He had the weight concession too, and we had some hardish races during the season.'

From the stands David Elsworth, who had no reason to suspect that the horse was below his best, watched the fall with some surprise.

'When he did fall he fell a bit novicey. He made a bit of a mistake, but one would be surprised if a little mistake like that would get him on the floor. But it did, and maybe that was his way of telling us that he'd had enough.

'I don't regret running him at Liverpool, but I think perhaps he was tired—mentally rather than physically. He'd had a great season, and you don't have a divine right to win everything.'

Sherwood felt he would have been beaten anyway. 'I would prefer that he had the fall and got away with it rather than finishing a tired fourth or fifth, which I think he would have done that day. So in his heart of hearts and in my heart of hearts we kept our unbeaten record together.'

One had to feel sorry for Yahoo and his connections after the race: the cameras and the eyes of the public

were focused largely on Desert Orchid as he was led back to the stables. Colin Brown, who usually finds the right words to sum up an occasion, did so again this time:

'Did you see the winner's enclosure as Yahoo was led in? It was about as busy as Ludlow after the 5.15 on a wet Wednesday evening!'

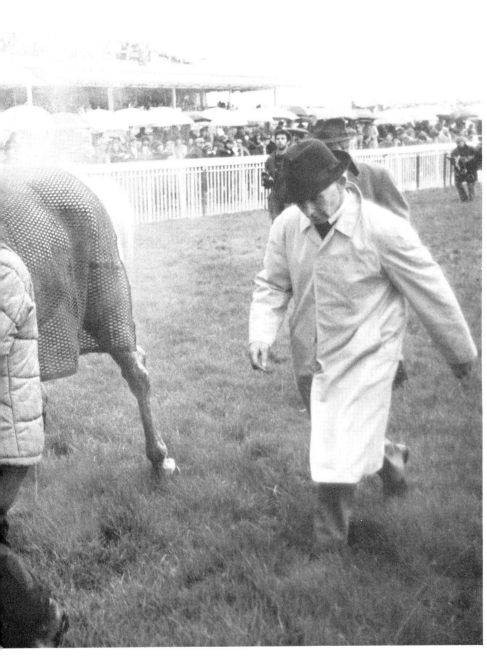

Concern on the faces
of Richard Burridge
and Janice Coyle
after Desert Orchid's
fall. Media attention
was focused more on
the grey horse than it
was on the race
winner, Yahoo.

Sum up

———

THREE WEEKS AFTER the fall at Liverpool, Simon Sherwood made public his decision to retire from race riding. He had negotiated the purchase of Roddy Armytage's old yard at East Ilsley, near Newbury, which he planned to rebuild before taking out a trainer's licence in 1990. And so a glorious chapter in the life of Desert Orchid came to an end, and the plum ride went to another naturally gifted big-race jockey—Richard Dunwoody. Sherwood was turning his back on some brilliant horses—Barnbrook Again and The West Awake as well as Desert Orchid—but the last two would have clashing commitments in the future and he no longer enjoyed the long hauls to Plumpton or Wolverhampton on a wet January Monday.

1988 had been a spectacular season. Apart from Liverpool, there had not been a single blot on the copybook, and Desert Orchid's popularity with the public had scaled unimaginable heights. In order to cope with the hundreds of requests from admirers for everything from photographs to hairs from the horse's tail, Richard Burridge formed the official Desert Orchid Fan Club, with all proceeds going to charity. The grey had become a national institution.

On 19 April Desert Orchid returned to Cheltenham, but not to race on this occasion. He was there to receive two Piper Champagne awards, one for the bravest horse in training, the other for the personality who has done the most for jump racing. He took centre stage in the parade ring like the star that he is, and his prize was an ice bucket full of his favourite mints. The occasion was a rare outing to the races for head lad Rodney Boult, who has always felt that his presence on the course put a jinx on Desert Orchid's performances.

At the Ibex, Colin Brown's cheerful and popular pub at Chaddleworth, there is a room called the Orchid Bar, given over to mementoes and photographs of the horse. Here, Brown and Sherwood, who in conversation refer to Desert Orchid rather irreverently as 'Desmond', are always happy to sit and talk about the grey, and Brown has known him since he was a three-year-old.

'I've always liked him—he always had a lot of character about him. Even when he was a baby and didn't get the trip and the ground was against him he was always tough and genuine and gave you his last drop of blood. He's got a lot of charisma, and you really become a friend of his.

'But I've noticed over the years that he always keeps his distance a bit—he's his own man, if you like. It doesn't matter who you are; if you go into his box and it doesn't suit him he sticks a foot upsides your ear to let you know that.'

Sherwood, who has seen the charisma and the respect in which the horse is held grow as he has won bigger and better races, is also a great admirer.

'He certainly has a certain amount of arrogance about him. I quite like relating horses to human beings, and I maintain that if Desert Orchid was a human being he would definitely have quite a flash sports car, and he would wear a blazer and no tie. He would be pretty relaxed about life, but things would come his way quite happily without him really trying. Possibly a bit of a poser. He enjoys his audience: he's a showman.

'Red Rum had tremendous charisma too, and he was also great horse—they are both the housewife's choice. But I think Desert Orchid has a wider appeal. Red Rum was essentially a Liverpool hero.'

Brown agrees. 'Everybody's heard of Desert Orchid, even people who are not interested in racing and have never been to a racecourse.

'Desert Orchid can win from two miles to three and

a half. Nothing's beyond him really. It was fantastic the way he came back at Sandown and Cheltenham to beat Pegwell Bay and Yahoo—makes your hair stand on end to watch it.

'I don't like comparing horses, and I never saw Arkle, but I've read all the books and I don't think Arkle would have won two miles to three and a half. And Red Rum was basically a Liverpool horse. I don't think that there has been anything as good or exciting as Desert Orchid for years.

'The other thing about Desert Orchid is how sound he is. He has never, ever, missed a day's work because of injury. Nowadays you could race him on any sort of ground from rock hard to heavy, because he acts on them all and he would probably beat them all on it.'

Certainly, the race-going public would love to see the grey repeat his stunning performances of that memorable 1988-89 season. However, Simon Sherwood has his doubts, and it is perhaps fitting that he should have the final word on this great horse.

'I think it's impossible. He won every major race he was entered for last season except the Martell Cup. Everything went pitter-patter for him as far as the ground was concerned, other than the Gold Cup.

'I'm sure he will win another King George, in fact he's a banker there. But as for the Gold Cup, I'm not so sure. It would be lovely to see him do it and I hope he can, but I think things will be more difficult next time.

'Having said that, I don't think he should be retired yet. As long as he carries on enjoying his races and stays in one piece and gives people a lot of thrills, he should keep going. He genuinely does love it, and his audience too.'

And so say half the nation. We shall probably never see his like again.

Desert Orchid's racing record

1982/83

KEMPTON	21 January			Good

Walton Novices' Hurdle		2 miles		£1,637
1 Boardman's Crown	4—11—0	M. Bastard	6-1	

made all after halfway, held on by short head

2 Butlers Pet	4—11—0	B. Wright	50-1	

lost place after halfway, but finished strongly

3 Busaco	4—11—0	M. Perrett	9-4 fav	

steady progress from halfway, every chance at last but one-paced on run-in
Desert Orchid—behind when fell last
18 RAN   DISTANCES: sh hd, 1, 1½

WINCANTON	24 February			Good

Mere Maiden Hurdle		2 miles		£645
1 Raise the Offer	4—10—10	J. Francome	12-1	

made most, kept on well

2 Hollymount	4—10—10	B. de Haan	10-1	

progress from halfway, every chance at last

3 Ikoyi Sunset	4—10—10	W. Smith	5-2 fav	

progress from three out, but lacked pace
Desert Orchid—no show, unplaced
22 RAN   DISTANCES: 1½, 5, 2

SANDOWN	11 March			Good

Lilac Novices' Hurdle (Div. 2)		2 miles		£1,265
1 Diamond Hunter	5—11—5	S. Smith Eccles	4-1	

led last, headed, regained advantage near finish

2 Desert Orchid	4—10—6	C. Brown	7-1	

good progress from 2 out, led last, beaten in final strides

3 Emperor Charles	6—11—5	B. de Haan	15-2	

led, mistakes at last two, found no extra
16 RAN   DISTANCES: nk, 3, 8

NEWBURY	25 March			Heavy

March Novices' Hurdle (Div. 2)   2 miles   £1,501

1 Appeljo	7—11—7	J. Lovejoy	20-1

first time out, led last, held on gamely

2 Destiny Bay	5—11—7	H. Davies	7-4 fav

kept on under pressure, just beaten

3 El Mansour	4—11—0	S. Smith Eccles	20-1

chance at last, out-paced

Desert Orchid—7th, chance 3
out, faded

14 RAN   DISTANCES: sh hd, 5, 3

1983/84

ASCOT	29 October			Firm

Haig Whisky Novices' Hurdle   2 miles   £1,931

1 Desert Orchid	4—10—10	C. Brown	11-8

made all, clear 3 out

2 Lucky Rascal	4—10—6	P. Double	5-4 fav

beaten 3 out

3 Sammy Lux	5—10—10	Mr P. Schofield	13-2

no danger

5 RAN   DISTANCES: 15, 20, 25

ASCOT	18 November			Firm

Bingley Novices' Hurdle   2 miles   £2,316

1 Desert Orchid	4—11—6	C. Brown	1-2 fav

made all

2 Don Giovanni	4—11—6	J. Francome	7-4

never threatened winner

3 Gillie's Prince	4—10—11	W. Morris	25-1

soon tailed off

3 RAN   DISTANCES: 15, 30

Desert Orchid puts in a superb jump in the early stages of the Gainsborough Handicap Chase at Sandown on 6 February 1987. He led or disputed the lead until two out, where the handicap of 12 stone finally anchored him.

SANDOWN	2 December			Firm

December Novices' Hurdle — 2 miles 5 furl — £4,885

1 Catch Phrase	5—11—4	R. Rowe	9-4	
ran on strongly to lead close to home				
2 Desert Orchid	4—11—3	C. Brown	5-6 fav	
made all until collared close to home				
3 Flash Fred	6—11—4	J. Lovejoy	16-1	
ran on but no threat				

9 RAN   DISTANCES: ¾, 10, 15

KEMPTON	26 December			Firm

Foodbrokers Armour Novices' Hurdle — 2 miles — £3,548

1 Desert Orchid	4—11—10	R. Linley	7-4 fav	
made all, unchallenged				
2 I Haventalight	4—10—10	J. Francome	5-2	
headway from 3 out, promising effort				
3 Derby Dilly	4—10—10	J. J. O'Neill	9-1	
ran on strongly				

10 RAN   DISTANCES: 15, 1, ½

SANDOWN	7 January			Good

Tolworth Hurdle — 2 miles — £4,482

1 Desert Orchid	5—11—11	C. Brown	5-6 fav	
made all, gave rivals no chance				
2 I Haventalight	5—11—7	J. Francome	4-1	
chased winner all the way, but in vain, finished well clear of the rest				
3 Horn of Plenty	5—11—7	H. Davies	50-1	
some late headway but never a threat				

6 RAN   DISTANCES: 8, 15, 2½

ASCOT	8 February			Good

Datchet Novices' Hurdle — 2 miles — £2,977

1 Desert Orchid	5—11—11	C. Brown	11-10 fav	
made all, never headed, stayed on strongly from 2 out				
2 Hill's Pageant	5—11—1	K. Mooney	12-1	
good hurdling debut, but one-pace from 2 out				
3 Brown Trix	6—11—5	J. Francome	7-1	
promising till no extra 2 out				

11 RAN   DISTANCES: 8, 12, 8

WINCANTON	23 February			Good

Kingwell Pattern Hurdle   2 miles   £6,059

1 Desert Orchid	5—11—2	C. Brown	2-1 fav

made all, kept on strongly from 2 out

2 Stans Pride	7—11—10	R. Crank	3-1

held up till challenged 3 out, mistake and no extra at last

3 Very Promising	6—11—12	B. de Haan	8-1

never seen until running on too late

9 RAN   DISTANCES: 4, 12, 2

CHELTENHAM	13 March			Good to Firm

Waterford Crystal Champion Hurdle   2 miles   £36,380

1 Dawn Run	6—11—9	J. J. O'Neill	4-5 fav

disputed lead throughout, responded well under pressure from 2 out

2 Cima	5—12—0	P. Scudamore	66-1

came with a strong challenge 2 out, just held

3 Very Promising	6—12—0	S. Morshead	16-1

chance 2 out, out-paced until running on late

Desert Orchid—7th, led briefly before halfway, never clear, soon beaten

14 RAN   DISTANCES: ¾, 4, 1½

1984/85

KEMPTON	20 October			Good to Firm

Captain Quist Hurdle   2 miles   £3,915

1 Ra Nova	5—11—10	M. Perrett	5-1

prominent, led after 2 out, held on well

2 Janus	6—11—4	R. Rowe	14-1

always prominent, ran well

3 Desert Orchid	5—11—10	C. Brown	2-1 fav

made all until headed 2 out

10 RAN   DISTANCES: 1½, 4, ½

ASCOT   15 December   Good

HSS Hire Shops Hurdle   2 miles   £4,819
1 See You Then   4—11—8   J. Francome   11-10 fav
came from behing to lead before last, driven out
2 Joy Ride   4—10—8   S. Smith Eccles   8-1
challenged 2 out, ran on bravely
3 Desert Orchid   5—11—8   C. Brown   5-1
disputed lead until 2 out
5 RAN   DISTANCES: 2, 5, 15

KEMPTON   26 December   Yielding

Ladbroke Christmas Hurdle   2 miles   £15,752
1 Browne's Gazette   6—11—3   D. Browne   11-8 fav
led after 2 out and won as he pleased
2 Desert Orchid   5—11—3   C. Brown   10-1
led until swamped for foot 2 out
3 See You Then   4—11—3   J. Francome   2-1
jumped stickily, beaten 2 out
7 RAN   DISTANCES: 15, 10, 8

LEOPARDSTOWN   12 January   Good

Irish Sweeps Handicap Hurdle   2 miles   £24,393
1 Hansel Rag   5—10—0   A. Powell   14-1
ran on steadily to lead before last
2 Bonalma   5—10—0   B. Sheridan   11-1
came to challenge at last
3 Another Shot   7—10—12   Mr T. Walsh
held up, finished well
Desert Orchid—9th, led until 2 out, ran wide on final bend
20 RAN   DISTANCES: 2½, 2, sh hd

SANDOWN		2 February			Soft

Oteley Hurdle — 2 miles — £4,417

1 Desert Orchid	6—11—5	C. Brown	2-1 fav

made all, clear halfway, won easily

2 Mr Moonraker	8—10—10	B. Powell	5-1

unable to challenge winner

3 Infielder	6—10—11	J. Francome	10-1

always prominent

8 RAN   DISTANCES: 10, 1½, ¾

CHELTENHAM		12 March			Firm

Waterford Crystal Champion Hurdle — 2 miles — £38,030

1 See You Then	5—12—0	S. Smith Eccles	16-1

always prominent, led after last and forged clear

2 Robin Wonder	7—12—0	J. J. O'Neill	66-1

finished very strongly

3 Stans Pride	8—11—9	S. Morshead	100-1

every chance at last

Desert Orchid—made very quick early pace, disputed lead, pulled up 2 out

16 RAN   DISTANCES: 7, 3, 1½

CHEPSTOW		8 April			Soft

Blue Circle Welsh Champion Hurdle — 2 miles — £8,480

1 Browne's Gazette	7—11—13	D. Browne	8-13 fav

improved steadily from halfway, led at last and ran on

2 Ra Nova	6—11—9	M. Perrett	9-1

led from 4 out till last, ran on well

3 Stans Pride	8—11—4	S. Morshead	5-1

every chance at last

Desert Orchid—blinkered first time, led till 4 out, soon beaten and pulled up

7 RAN   DISTANCES: 1½, 3, ¾

ASCOT	13 April		Good

Trillium Handicap Hurdle 2 miles £3,833

1 Comedy Fair 5—10—5 J. J. O'Neill 7-4 fav

under strong pressure, 2 lengths behind when left in lead at last by fall of Desert Orchid

2 Rhythmic Pastimes 5—10—12 S. Smith Eccles 5-1

always prominent

3 Mister Golden 5—10—1 J. Duggan 100-30

ran in snatches, finished well, clear of rest

Desert Orchid—made all, 2 lengths clear when fell at last

8 RAN DISTANCES: 1½, 1½, 10

1985/86

KEMPTON	19 October		Firm

Captain Quist Hurdle 2 miles £3,830

1 Wing and a Prayer 4—11—3 S. Sherwood 7-2

well beaten in 2nd when left clear 2 out, tenderly ridden

2 Life Guard 4—11—3 J. Frost 25-1

out-paced in rear till ridden and ran on well from 2 out

3 Monza 7—10—9 R. Rowe 13-2

prominent, out-paced 3 out, no extra

Desert Orchid—led, clear 3 out, easy winner when falling 2 out

6 RAN DISTANCES: 1½, 10, 20

DEVON AND EXETER	1 November		Good to Firm

Woolea Lambskin Products Ltd Novice's Chase 2 miles 1 furlong £1,607

1 Desert Orchid 6—11—0 C. Brown 4-5 fav

first time over fences, made all, came home unchallenged

2 Charcoal Wally 6—11—7 R. Linley 6-5

always 2nd but no chance with winner

3 Pridden Jimmy 6—11—0 B. Wright 33-1

never near first 2

5 RAN DISTANCES: 25, dist., 25

ASCOT	15 November			Firm

Hurst Park Novices' Chase 2 miles £7,987

1 Desert Orchid	6—11—4	C. Brown	4-9 fav

made every yard, jumped well, won at a canter

2 Cocaine	7—11—4	C. Mann	9-2

kept with winner until out-paced on home turn

3 Yacare	6—11—4	R. Rowe	7-1

chasing debut
4 RAN DISTANCES: 12, dist., 2

SANDOWN	30 November			Good

Henry VIII Novices' Chase 2 miles £3,579

1 Desert Orchid	6—11—4	C. Brown	4-11 fav

made all, never threatened

2 Taffy Jones	6—10—12	P. Barton	5-1

creditable run

3 Evening Song	6—10—7	R. Goldstein	33-1

always there, never threatened leader
5 RAN DISTANCES: 7, 5, 8

ASCOT	14 December			Good to Firm

Killiney Novices' Chase 2 miles 4 furl £5,638

1 Desert Orchid	6—11—11	C. Brown	5-4 fav

jumped well in lead, survived blunder 3 out to win unchallenged

2 Evening Song	6—10—7	R. Goldstein	50-1

stayed on well, but no impression on winner

3 Play Boy	6—10—12	J. Duggan	3-1

lost place over 6 out, stayed on again
6 RAN DISTANCES: 20, 4, 10

ASCOT	10 January			Good to Soft

Thunder and Lightning Novices' Chase 2 miles £7,036

1 Pearlyman	7—11—4	P. Barton	5-1

left clear 3 out by falls of both other runners

2 Charcoal Wally	7—11—4	G. McCourt	5-1

in lead halfway, fell 3 out, remounted for second place
Desert Orchid—clear lead when unseated rider 5th
3 RAN DISTANCES: not taken

SANDOWN 1 February Soft, heavy patches

Scilly Isles Novices' Chase 2 miles £7,680
1 Berlin 7—11—10 D. Browne 5-2
led 3 out and battled on well
2 Desert Orchid 7—11—10 C. Brown 10-11 fav
made most until mistake 3 out, rallied on run-in, just held
3 Allten Glazed 9—11—5 G. Bradley 7-1
faded after last
6 RAN DISTANCES: ½, 15, hd

CHELTENHAM 11 March Good to Soft

Arkle Challenge Trophy 2 miles £21,215
1 Oregan Trail 6—11—8 R. J. Beggan 14-1
headway 6th, responded to strong driving to lead on post
2 Charcoal Wally 7—11—8 B. Powell 11-1
chased leader, went on 3 out, caught on line
3 Desert Orchid 7—11—8 C. Brown 11-2
set a fast pace till 3 out
14 RAN DISTANCES: ¾, 8, 8

SANDOWN 25 March Good

British Aerospace Rapier Novices' Chase 2 miles 4 furl £3,993
1 Clara Mountain 7—11—8 H. Davies 2-1
under pressure last, ran on well to lead
2 Desert Orchid 7—11—8 C. Brown 10-11 fav
made most till last, clear of rest
3 Whiskey Eyes 5—10—9 M. Harrington 5-1
every chance, did not quicken
6 RAN DISTANCES: 1½, 15, 20

ASCOT	12 April		Good to Firm

Contiboard Novices' Handicap Chase   2 miles 4 furl   £11,107
1 Repington   8—10—3   C. Hawkins   9-1
chased leader till went on after 2 out
2 Just Alick   7—10—0   K. Mooney   10-1
soon prominent, good effort
3 Garfunkel   7—10—3   R. Dunwoody   14-1
prominent, mistake 4 out, kept on
Desert Orchid—5th, set blinding pace until blundered 4 out, headed before last
13 RAN   DISTANCES: 6, 2½, ¾

1986/87

SANDOWN	1 November		Good

Holsten Export Lager Handicap Chase   2 miles 4 furl   £4,950
1 Desert Orchid   7—10—3   C. Brown   7-4 jt fav
made every yard, quickened from last for comfortable win
2 The Argonaut   8—10—0   S. Shilston   9-4
mistake 6 out, challenged last
3 Very Promising   8—12—0   R. Dunwoody   7-4 jt fav
every chance nearing last
4 RAN   DISTANCES: 4, 3, dist.

ASCOT	15 November		Good to Firm

H & T Walker Goddess Handicap Chase   2 miles 4 furl   £18,584
1 Church Warden   7—10—7   R. Dunwoody   12-1
first time out, came from well off the pace to lead final 100 yards
2 Berlin   7—11—0   D. Browne   9-2
hit front 4 out but ran out of it close to home
3 Amber Rambler   7—11—5   R. Rowe   9-2
challenged 2 out, no extra
Desert Orchid—4th, never in front, no extra at last
6 RAN   DISTANCES: 1½, 4, hd

ASCOT	13 December			Good

Frogmore Handicap Chase 2 miles £6,801

1 Desert Orchid 7—11—5 C. Brown 7-2 jt fav
disputed lead throughout, drew clear comfortably approaching last
2 Charcoal Wally 7—11—3 B. Powell 4-1
led or disputed lead from halfway until 2 out
3 Little Bay 11—11—10 P. Tuck 7-2 jt fav
came from behind, no extra from last
8 RAN DISTANCES: 12, 2½, hd

KEMPTON	26 December			Soft

King George VI Rank Chase 3 miles £31,696

1 Desert Orchid 7—11—10 S. Sherwood 16-1
made every yard at fast pace, never in danger, comfortable winner
2 Door Latch 8—11—10 R. Rowe 10-1
tracked leader most of the way but no chance
3 Bolands Cross 7—11—10 P. Scudamore 9-2
always prominent, ran to his best
9 RAN DISTANCES: 15, 6, 1

SANDOWN	7 February			Good

FU's Jeans Gainsborough Handicap Chase 3 miles £15,666

1 Desert Orchid 8—11—10 C. Brown 11-4
made all, drew clear from 3 out to win at fast pace
2 Stearsby 8—11—4 G. McCourt 3-1
minor errors, lacked pace of winner
3 Bolands Cross 8—11—0 P. Scudamore 9-4 fav
always prominent, bad mistake at water 2nd time and hampered 2 out
6 RAN DISTANCES: 10, 3, 12

WINCANTON	26 February			Good to Soft

Jim Ford Challenge Cup 3 miles 1 furl £6,322

1 Desert Orchid 8—11—11 C. Brown 1-2 fav
soon led, one mistake, easy winner
2 Mr Moonraker 10—11—7 B. Powell 4-1
well ahead of other two
3 Fire Drill 12—11—7 P. Richards 50-1
outclassed
4 RAN DISTANCES: 12, dist., 15

CHELTENHAM   18 March   Good

Queen Mother Champion Chase   2 miles   £25,775
1 Pearlyman   8—12—0   P. Scudamore   13-8 fav
made good headway to challenge 2 out, slight mistake last 2 fences, got up in final
100 yards
2 Very Promising   9—12—0   R. Dunwoody   3-1
always going well, led approaching last, just ran out of it in final stages
3 Desert Orchid   8—12—0   C. Brown   9-4
set fast pace, headed after 2 out, lost nothing in defeat
8 RAN   DISTANCES: nk, 3, 25

ASCOT   8 April   Good to Soft

Peregrine Handicap Chase   2 miles 4 furl   £7,142
1 Desert Orchid   8—12—4   C. Brown   7-4 fav
led till mistake 4 out, came again bravely, forged on from last
2 Gold Bearer   7—10—0   P. Scudamore   33-1
19 lbs out of handicap, but led 4 out and only headed at last
3 Sign Again   9—10—3   R. Dunwoody   10-1
never threatened first two
7 RAN   DISTANCES: 2, 3, 2½

SANDOWN   25 April   Firm

Whitbread Gold Cup   3 miles 5 furl   £32,250
1 Lean Ar Aghaidh   10—10—0   G. Landau   6-1
made all, stayed gamely on despite bad blunder 6 out
2 Contradeal   10—10—0   K. Mooney   5-1
progress from halfway, every chance approaching last, stayed on well
3 Broadheath   10—10—6   P. Nicholls   14-1
looked dangerous 3 out, but no extra from next
Desert Orchid—never going or jumping well, behind when pulled up 5 out
9 RAN   DISTANCES: 5, 7, 6

1987/88

WINCANTON	29 October			Good

Terry Biddlecombe Challenge Trophy   2 miles 5 furl   £3,842

1 Desert Orchid	8—11—8	C. Brown	1-7 fav

made all, jumped well, easy win

2 Sugar Bee	9—11—8	H. Davies	6-1

jumped well but never a threat

3 Britannicus	11—11—1	D. Morris	25-1

totally outclassed

3 RAN   DISTANCES: dist., dist.

KEMPTON	18 November			Good to Soft

Rank Boxing Day Trial Chase   2 miles 4 furl   £7,502

1 Desert Orchid	8—11—10	C. Brown	1-5 fav

made every yard to win as he pleased

2 Bishops Yarn	8—10—10	R. Guest	7-1

held up, took 2nd after last

3 Galway Blaze	11—10—10	S. Sherwood	8-1

2nd until after the last, needed the race

3 RAN   DISTANCES: 12, 1

SANDOWN	5 December			Good

Tingle Creek Handicap Chase   2 miles   £8,796

1 Long Engagement	6—10—2	R. Dunwoody	3-1

always going well, led 2 out and quickened well after last

2 Desert Orchid	8—12—0	C. Brown	10-11 fav

led or disputed throughout, anchored by 12 stone from 2 out

3 Amber Rambler	8—10—0	B. Walsh	5-1

prominent till 3 out

5 RAN   DISTANCES: 3, 15, 20

KEMPTON	26 December			Good

King George VI Rank Chase   3 miles   £31,400

1 Nupsala (Fr)   8—11—10   A. Pommier   25-1
always going well, took lead 2 out, left clear at last

2 Desert Orchid   8—11—10   C. Brown   evens fav
involved in breakneck battle for lead from start, no more to give from 3 out

3 Golden Friend   9—11—10   D. Browne   20-1
outpaced until staying on late
9 RAN   DISTANCES: 15, 3, 1

SANDOWN	6 February			Heavy

Lee Cooper Gainsborough Handicap Chase   3 miles   £20,450

1 Charter Party   10—10—11   R. Dunwoody   100-30 fav
always prominent, led after 2 out to win comfortably

2 Rhyme 'N' Reason   9—10—7   B. Powell   7-2
outpaced early, stayed on well under pressure from 2 out

3 Desert Orchid   9—12—0   C. Brown   7-2
led or disputed lead until 2 out, anchored by 12 stone up final hill
11 RAN   DISTANCES: 8, nk, 12

WINCANTON	25 February			Good to Soft

Jim Ford Challenge Cup   3 miles 1 furl   £7,527

1 Kildimo   8—11—11   G. Bradley   2-1
tracked leader all the way and collared him at the last

2 Desert Orchid   9—11—11   C. Brown   1-2 fav
set modest pace, headed last

3 Burrough Hill Lad   12—11—11   R. Rowe   9-1
first run for two years, always in touch but mistakes when tiring at last 2
3 RAN   DISTANCES: 1½, dist.

CHELTENHAM	16 March			Heavy

Queen Mother Champion Chase   2 miles   £39,869

1 Pearlyman   9—12—0   T. Morgan   15-8 fav
always travelling well, sent on approaching last

2 Desert Orchid   9—12—0   C. Brown   9-1
led until 2 out, came on bravely to snatch 2nd, lost nothing in defeat

3 Very Promising   10—12—0   R. Dunwoody   4-1
rallied well under pressure, went 2nd approaching last, tired close to home
8 RAN   DISTANCES: 5, 1, 2½

LIVERPOOL	7 April			Good

Chivas Regal Cup — 3 miles 1 furl — £16,040

1 Desert Orchid	9—11—5	S. Sherwood	3-1

made all, jumped well, first success on left-handed track

2 Kildimo	8—11—5	G. Bradley	2-1 fav

2nd from halfway, no extra from 3 out

3 Weather the Storm	8—11—13	T. J. Taafe	8-1

mistakes, weakened 5 out

4 RAN DISTANCES: 8, 12, dist.

SANDOWN	23 April			Good to Firm

Whitbread Gold Cup — 3 miles 5 furl — £45,000

1 Desert Orchid	9—11—11	S. Sherwood	6-1

made most, jumped well, quickened on run-in

2 Kildimo	8—11—12	J. Frost	6-1

steady headway, challenged winner 2 out, led briefly, out-battled from last

3 Strands of Gold	9—10—0	P. Scudamore	6-1

challenged after 3 out, mistake next, no extra

12 RAN DISTANCES: 2½, 4, 6

1988/89

WINCANTON	27 October			Good

Terry Biddlecombe Challenge Trophy — 2 miles 5 furl — £3,694

1 Desert Orchid	9—11—8	S. Sherwood	2-7 fav

made all, jumped well, won as he pleased

2 Bishops Yarn	9—11—8	R. Guest	9-1

held up in rear, ran on well, but never a threat to winner

3 Golden Friend	10—11—8	D. Browne	5-1

jumped well, just failed to hold 2nd

5 RAN DISTANCES: 15, ½

SANDOWN   3 December   Good

Tingle Creek Handicap Chase   2 miles   £8,812
1 Desert Orchid   9—12—0   S. Sherwood   5-2
made every yard, defied 12 stone to run on well up hill, won easily
2 Jim Thorpe   7—10—8   M. Dwyer   3-1
in touch, blundered third and fourth, rallied well approaching last
3 Panto Prince   7—10—10   B. Powell   4-1
in touch, every chance until ridden and outpaced after two out
5 RAN   DISTANCES: 12, ½, dist.

KEMPTON   26 December   Good to Firm

King George VI Rank Chase   3 miles   £37,280
1 Desert Orchid   9—11—10   S. Sherwood   1-2 fav
led to 10th, led again from 12th, stayed on strongly
2 Kildimo   8—11—10   J. Frost   8-1
in touch, every chance from 3 out, one-paced after last
3 Vodkatini   9—11—10   Peter Hobbs   7-1
led after 10th, headed 12th, every chance 3 out but one-paced
5 RAN   DISTANCES: 4, 5, 4

ASCOT   14 January   Good

Victor Chandler Handicap Chase   2 miles   £21,949
1 Desert Orchid   10—12—0   S. Sherwood   6-4 fav
led 3rd, headed after 5th, disputed lead last, headed again on run-in, rallied to lead at post
2 Panto Prince   8—10—6   B. Powell   3-1
led after 5th, quickened approach 2 out, led run in, caught post
3 Ida's Delight   10—10—0   P. Dennis   66-1
lost touch 7th, stayed on well from 2 out
5 RAN   DISTANCES: hd, 8, 10

SANDOWN   4 February   Good

Racecall Gainsborough Handicap Chase   3 miles   £19,340
1 Desert Orchid   10—12—0   S. Sherwood   6-5 fav
led to 12th, steadied, led briefly last, headed run-in, fought back to lead near finish
2 Pegwell Bay   8—10—10   C. Llewellyn   4-1
tracked winner from 2nd, led 12th, ran on, headed close to home
3 Kildimo   9—10—13   J. Frost   2-1
held up, mistakes 13th and 14th, made headway, every chance 2 out, outpaced run-in
4 RAN   DISTANCES: ¾, 2½, 25

CHELTENHAM 16 March Heavy

Tote Cheltenham Gold Cup 3 miles 2 furl £68,371
1 Desert Orchid 10—12—0 S. Sherwood 5-2
led to 14th, left in lead 3 out, headed, quickened to lead again on run-in
2 Yahoo 8—12—0 T. Morgan 25-1
well in touch, led approaching 2 out, headed under pressure on run-in
3 Charter Party 11—12—0 R. Dunwoody 14-1
always with leaders, every chance 3 out, one-paced but kept on gamely
13 RAN DISTANCES: 1½, 8, dist.

LIVERPOOL 6 April Soft

Martell Cup Chase 3 miles 1 furl £33,990
1 Yahoo 8—11—5 T. Morgan 5-1
held up, headway 12th, ran on well
2 Delius 11—11—5 B. Dowling 12-1
left in lead 12th, headed run-in, no extra
3 Bishops Yarn 10—11—5 R. Guest 13-1
progress from 13th, no extra from 15th
Desert Orchid—made all until fell 12th
8 RAN DISTANCES: 10, 10, 2½

Desert Orchid

Races 55: Won 27: 2nd 9: 3rd 5: fell 4
Total 1st prize money earnings: £349,134.25
Total overall prize money earnings: £408,107.61 (National Hunt record)
Jockeys: R. Linley—1 ride, 1 win
        C. Brown—43 rides, 17 wins
        S. Sherwood—10 rides, 9 wins
Bred by James Burridge, owned by Richard Burridge
Trained by David Elsworth, Fordingbridge, Hampshire